PIANO • VOCAL • GUITAR

THE LIN-MANUEL
MIRANDA
COLLECTION

Cover photo © The Washington Post / Contributor

978-1-70516-552-2

Visit Hal Leonard Online at
www.halleonard.com

World headquarters, contact:
Hal Leonard
7777 West Bluemound Road
Milwaukee, WI 53213
Email: info@halleonard.com

In Europe, contact:
Hal Leonard Europe Limited
1 Red Place
London, W1K 6PL
Email: info@halleonardeurope.com

In Australia, contact:
Hal Leonard Australia Pty. Ltd.
4 Lentara Court
Cheltenham, Victoria, 3192 Australia
Email: info@halleonard.com.au

You write for a character, in a moment.

You think about where your character is at **THIS** moment, where they've been. You consider your character's pulse, temperament, upbringing. You think about the music they like, their world, the things they know. Then you put yourself in their shoes and figure out what they're aching to sing. What **ONLY** they can express in that moment. You sit at the piano. Or you take a walk in the park with your dog. You sing to yourself. When it feels true, you write it down, and little by little, draft by draft, you feel your way towards the song.

You share the song with your trusted collaborators. Their reactions and input send you back to the piano to rewrite, to make each moment in your song truer and clearer.

You do that over and over again, with every character you help to write.

And if you're very lucky, one day you look up, and your characters are all still there, and they're alive as long as someone is singing their songs. Your songs. Enough to fill a book.

Thank you to Quiara Alegría Hudes, Tom Kitt, Amanda Green, Jeff Whitty, Kirk DeMicco, Jared Bush, Charise Castro Smith, Opetaia Foa'i, Mark Mancina, and Germaine Franco, the writers who created the moments in this book alongside me.

Thank you to Tommy Kail, Andy Blankenbuehler, Michael Mayer, Jon M. Chu, Ron Clements and John Musker, and Byron Howard, directors who facilitated the shared visions for these moments to arrive.

Thank you to Bill Sherman, Alex Lacamoire, Michael Starobin, and Mike Elizondo, and all the arrangers and orchestrators I've been lucky enough to work with (with an extra special thanks to Lac for helping proofread the notes in this book you're holding).

Thank you to the casts of *In the Heights*, *Bring It On: The Musical*, *21 Chump Street*, *Hamilton*, *Moana*, *Vivo* & *Encanto*—your incredible voices helped find these characters' voices every step of the way.

Thank you to Vanessa Nadal, who has the best musical instincts of anyone I know.

Thank you to Sebastian and Francisco Miranda, the best beta testers around.

Thank you to Luz and Luis Miranda for all the piano lessons and cast albums, and Luz Miranda-Crespo for letting me raid her music collection throughout our childhood.

Thanks to everyone at Team Miranda, who carve out space for me every day to daydream and write.

And thank you to Tobillo Miranda, my dog, who has endured more first drafts in process than anyone in the family.

Finally, to Nina, Usnavi, Vanessa, Abuela Claudia and everyone on your block uptown; Campbell, Danielle, Nautica & La Cienega and the residents of Jackson and Truman High; Justin & Naomi (and your cousin); Aaron Burr, Alexander, Eliza, Angelica (& Peggy), and everyone who tells your story; Moana & Maui & the residents of Motu-Nui; Vivo & Andres and Gabi, and every animal from Havana to Miami; the incredible Familia Madrigal and your encanto, and all the other characters in these pages: Thank you for whispering to me what you were aching to sing. I did my best to get it all.

Siempre,
Lin-Manuel Miranda

CONTENTS BY SONG

CONTENTS BY SHOW

ALEXANDER HAMILTON

from HAMILTON

Words and Music by
LIN-MANUEL MIRANDA

lot smart-er, by be-ing a self - start-er, by four - teen, they placed him in charge of a trad-ing char-ter. And ev-'ry day while slaves were be-ing slaugh-tered and cart-ed a-way___ a-cross the waves, he strug-gled and kept his guard up. In-side, he was long-ing for some-thing to be a part of, the broth - er was read-y to beg, steal,_ bor-row or bar-ter. Then a hur-ri-cane came, and dev-as-ta-tion reigned, our man___ saw his fu-ture drip, drip-ping down the drain, put a

BREATHE
from IN THE HEIGHTS

Music and Lyrics by LIN-MANUEL MIRANDA
Arrangement by ALEX LACAMOIRE
and BILL SHERMAN

PIRAGUA GUY: Sig - ue an - dan - do el ca - mi - no por to - da su vi - da. ___ Res - pi - ra... ___

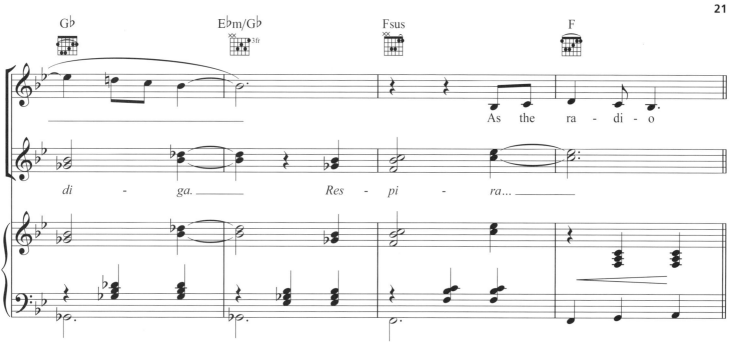

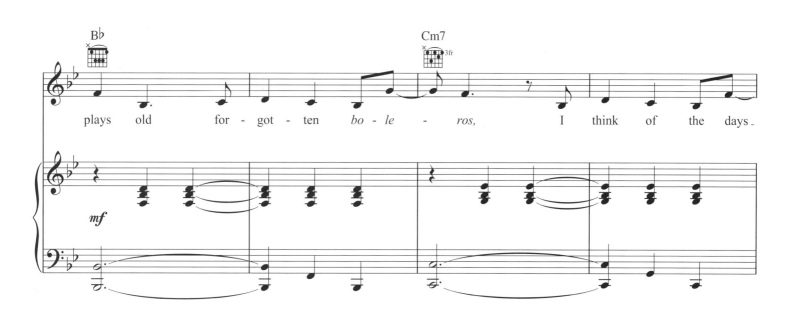

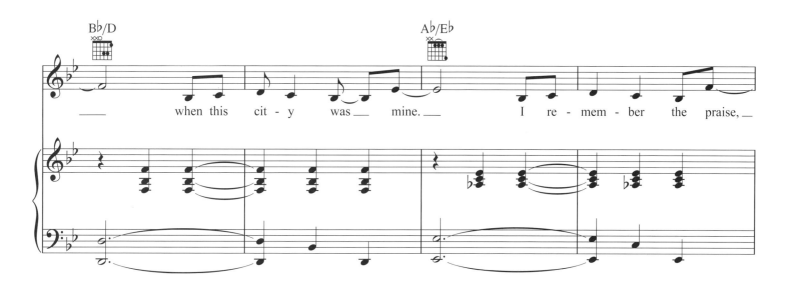

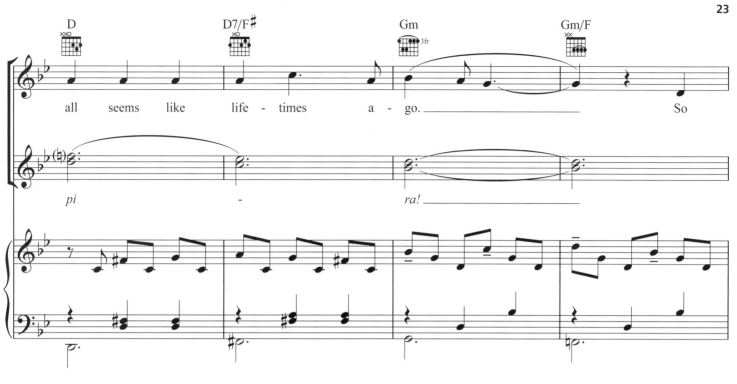

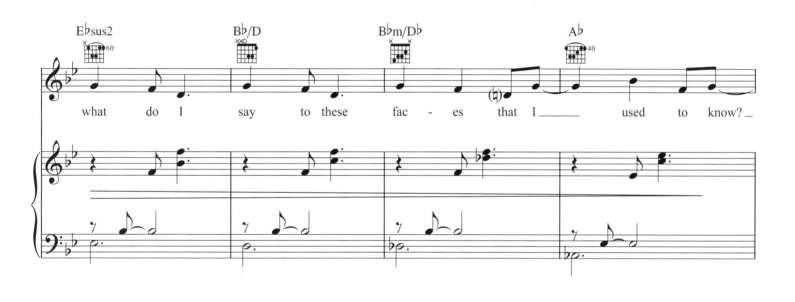

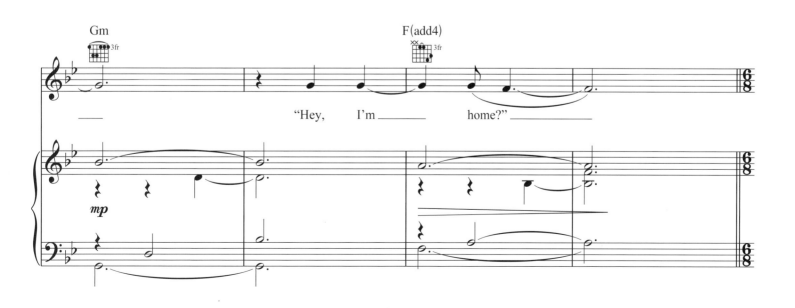

24

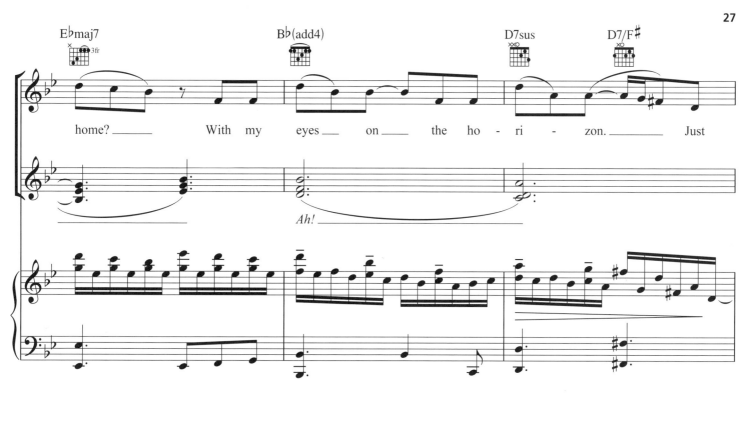

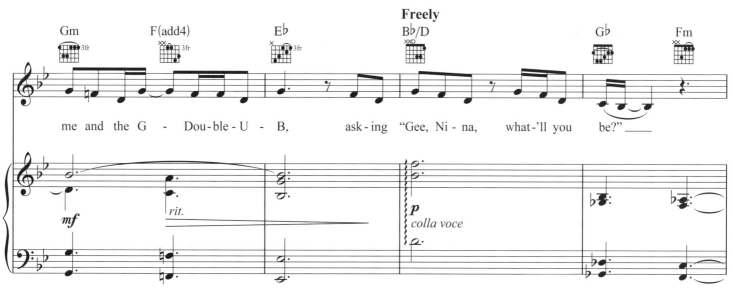

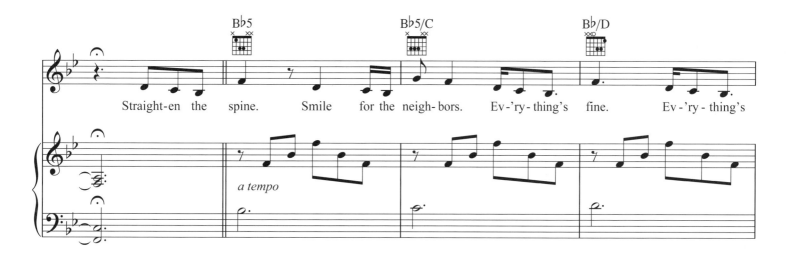

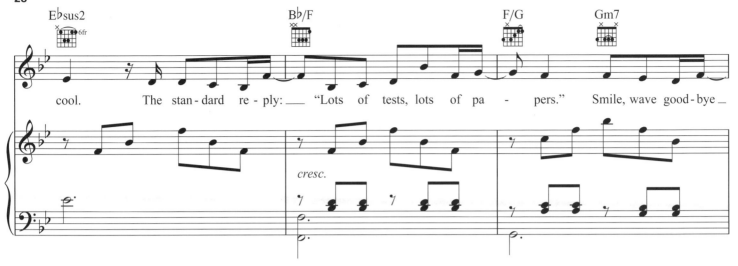

cool. The stan-dard re-ply:___ "Lots of tests, lots of pa - pers." Smile, wave good-bye___

___ and pray to the sky. Oh, God!___ And what will my par-ents say?___

Can I___ go in there___ and say,___ "I

COMMUNITY:

Ni - na...   Ni - na...

know that I'm let-ting you down"? _____

Freely, colla voce   **Tempo I**

CLAUDIA: NINA:

Ni - na...   Just   breathe. _____

No pedal

Add pedal

rall.

COUSIN

from 21 CHUMP STREET

Words and Music by
LIN-MANUEL MIRANDA

Driving

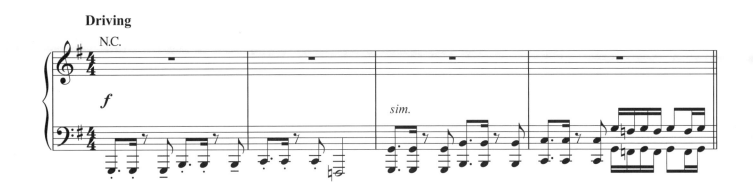

JUSTIN:

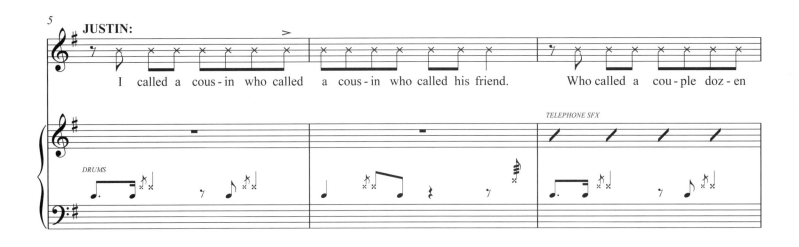

I called a cous-in who called a cous-in who called his friend. Who called a cou-ple doz-en

COUSIN 1:

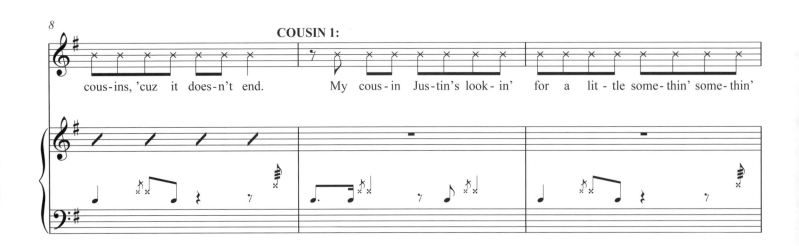

cous-ins, 'cuz it does-n't end. My cous-in Jus-tin's look-in' for a lit-tle some-thin' some-thin'

DO YOUR OWN THING

from BRING IT ON

Words and Music by
LIN-MANUEL MIRANDA

somebody, anyone show me around? _____

STUDENTS:
Hey! _____

STUDENTS:
Don't follow me! Why you on top of me? Leave me alone! _ Do your own _

_ thing, Ho! _____ Do your own _____ thing! Hey! _____

TEACHER'S VOICE:
Class, please welcome a new transfer student from Truman High.
Please give a warm Jackson welcome to—uh, what's her name—Campbell?

CAMPBELL: *Campbell.*
CAMERON: *Like the soup?*
TWIG: *Lookin' hot, Cream of Mushroom!*

BRIDGET: *Campbell!*
CAMPBELL: *Bridget! Thank God!*
BRIDGET: *O-M-Goodness, you got redistricted too?*
CAMPBELL: *Can you believe this?*
BRIDGET: *I'm in heaven. I bet I've got until lunch at least before everyone sees I'm a spaz!*
CAMPBELL: *I wish Steven was here. I'm so not used to not fitting in.*

BRIDGET: *Oh, I've got lots of experience with not fitting in.*
Do you need some pointers?
CAMPBELL: *I guess.*
BRIDGET: *Okay.*

TWIG: *Lookin' fine, baby.* BRIDGET: *Sorry, what?* TWIG: *I say you lookin' fine!*

BRIDGET: *Jinkies, no one has EVER SAID THAT to me before—with the exception of a hobo, once, and my youth pastor.*

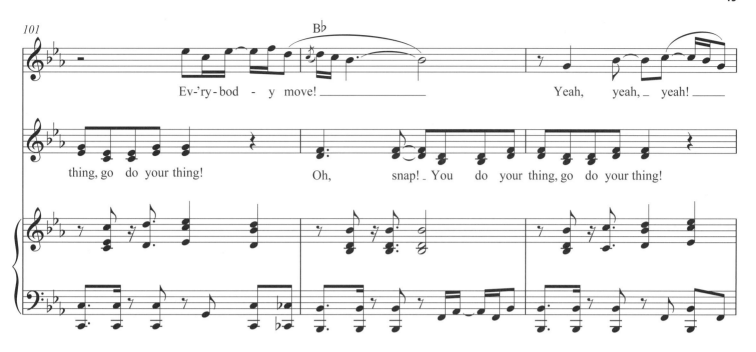

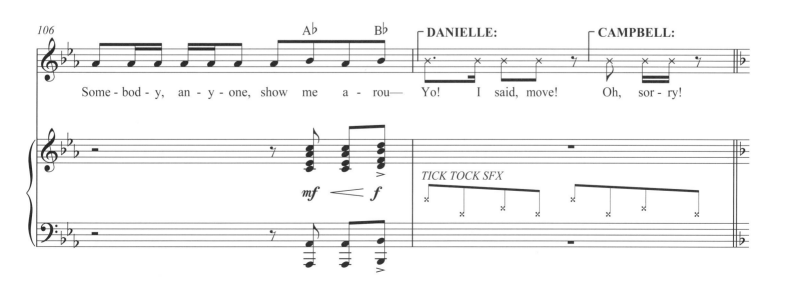

DOS ORUGUITAS

from ENCANTO

Music and Lyrics by
LIN-MANUEL MIRANDA

Syncopated groove

Dos or - u - gui - tas,   e - na - mo - ra - das,
Dos or - u - gui - tas   pa - ran el vien - to,

pa - san sus no - ches   y ma - dru - ga - das.
mien - tras se a - bra - zan   con sen - ti - mien - to.

Lle - nas de ham - bre,   si - guen an - dan - do ____ y
Si - guen cre - cien - do,   no sa - ben cuán - do ____ bu -

* *Lead vocal melody 2nd/3rd time.*

* *Lead vocal melody 3rd time.*

THE FAMILY MADRIGAL
from ENCANTO

Music and Lyrics by
LIN-MANUEL MIRANDA

N.C.

TOWN KIDS: *Oh my gosh, it's them!*   *But I don't know who is who?*   **MIRABEL:** *Alright, alright, relax.*
What are the gifts?! I can't remember all the gifts.

Percussion continues

TOWN KIDS: *It is physically impossible to relax! Tell us everything! What are your powers?*

D.S. al Coda

TOWN KID:
JUST TELL US WHAT EVERYONE CAN DO!   **MIRABEL:** *And that's why coffee's for grownups.*

end percussion

CODA

Db   Abm   Gb

- ri - gal! ___   Two guys ___ fell in love with Fam - ily Mad-
     (Hey Fam - ily Mad-

G♭

A♭

**TOWN KIDS &
TOWNSPEOPLE:**

grand - kid round up! Grand - kid round up!

D♭   G♭   D♭

MIRABEL: Cous - in Do - lor - es can hear a pin _____ drop...

A♭   D♭   G♭   A♭

Ca - mi - lo shape _____ shifts, An - ton - i - o gets _____ his gift _____ to - day!

D♭

My old - er sis - - ters, Is - a - bel - a and Lui - sa...
TOWNSPEOPLE: (Is - a - bel - a and Lui - sa!)

HELPLESS

from HAMILTON

Words and Music by
LIN-MANUEL MIRANDA

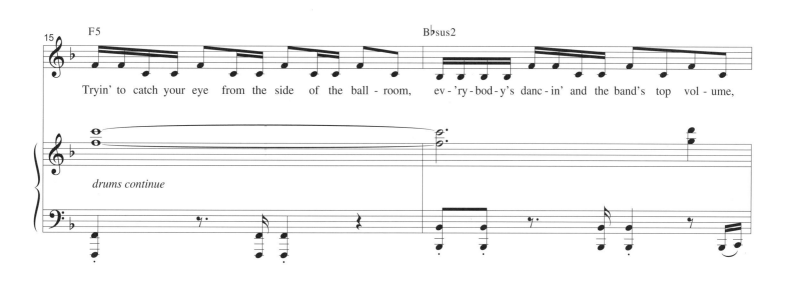

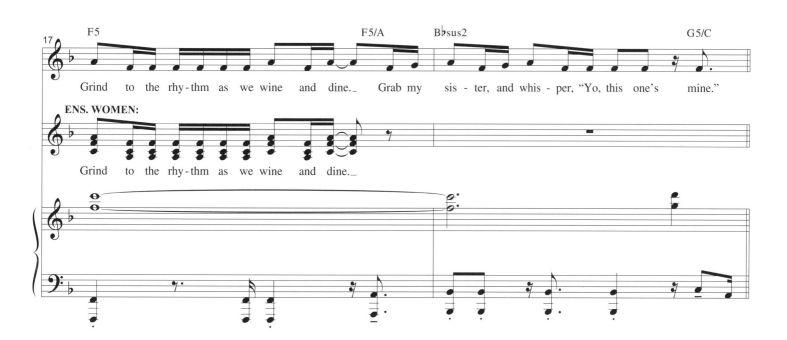

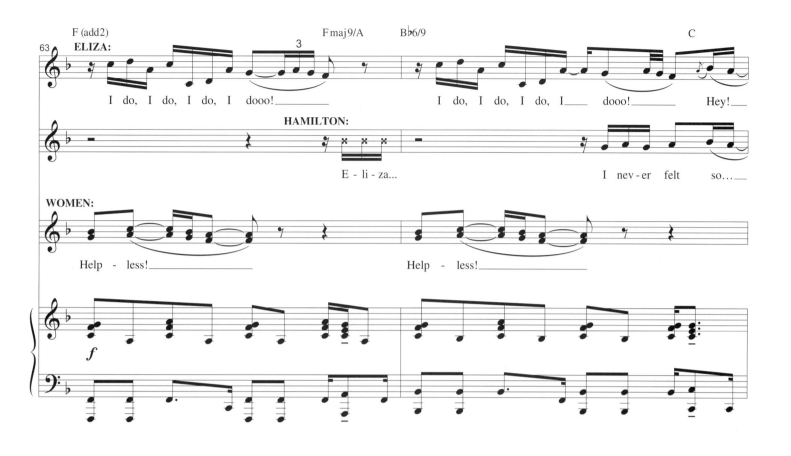

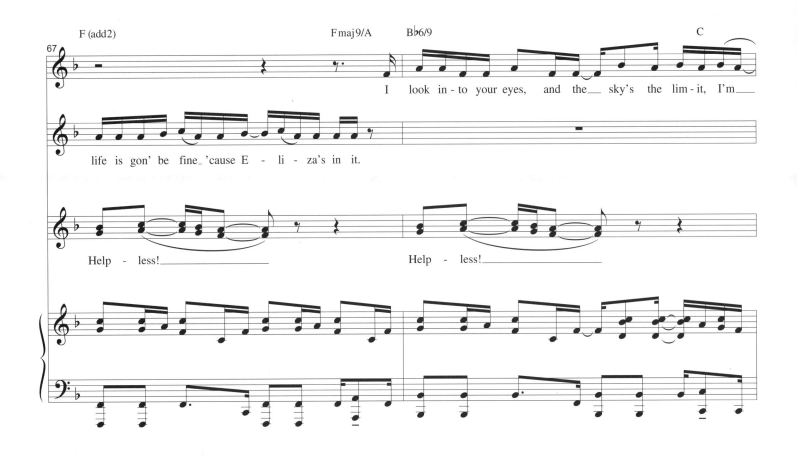

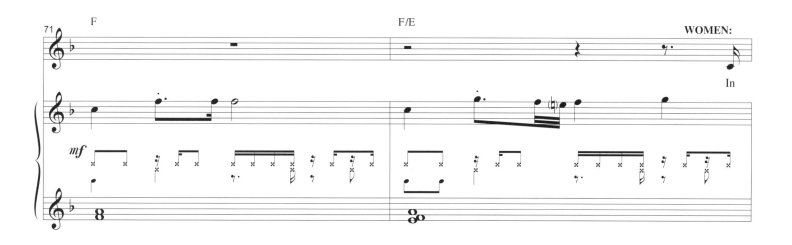

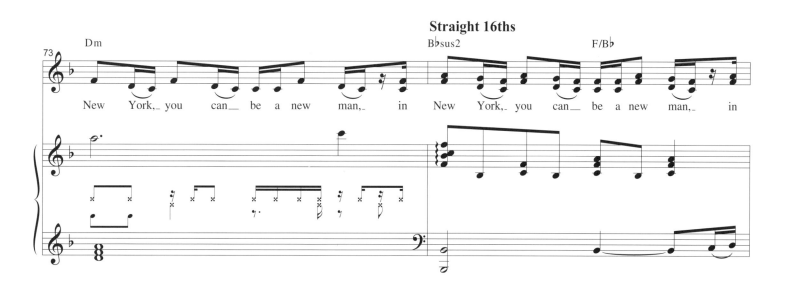

HOW FAR I'LL GO

from MOANA

Music and Lyrics by
LIN-MANUEL MIRANDA

IN THE HEIGHTS

from IN THE HEIGHTS

Music and Lyrics by LIN-MANUEL MIRANDA
Arrangement by ALEX LACAMOIRE
and BILL SHERMAN

Hip-Hop, half-time feel

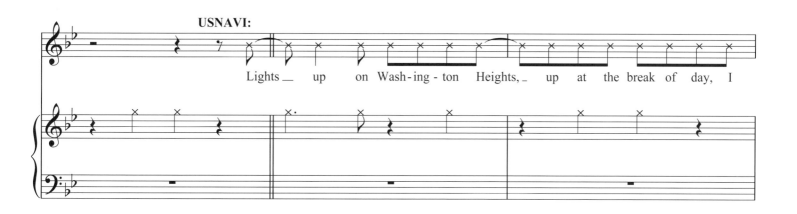

USNAVI: Lights __ up on Wash-ing-ton Heights, __ up at the break of day, I

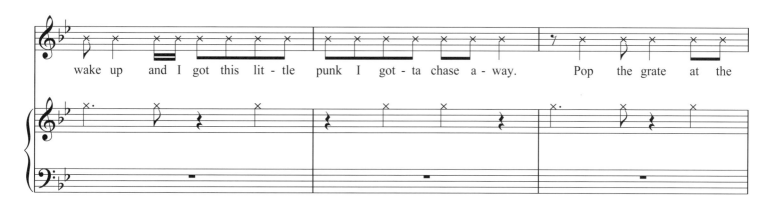

wake up and I got this lit-tle punk I got-ta chase a-way. Pop the grate at the

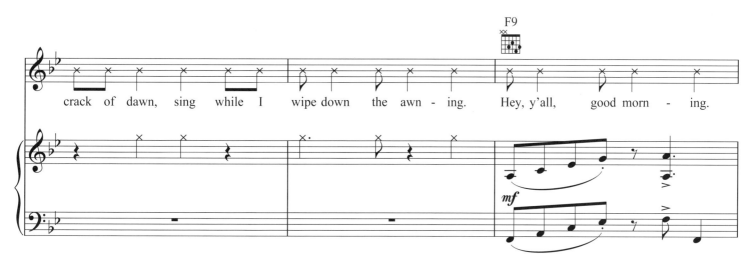

crack of dawn, sing while I wipe down the awn-ing. Hey, y'all, good morn - ing.

INSIDE YOUR HEART

from the feature film VIVO

Music and Lyrics by
LIN-MANUEL MIRANDA

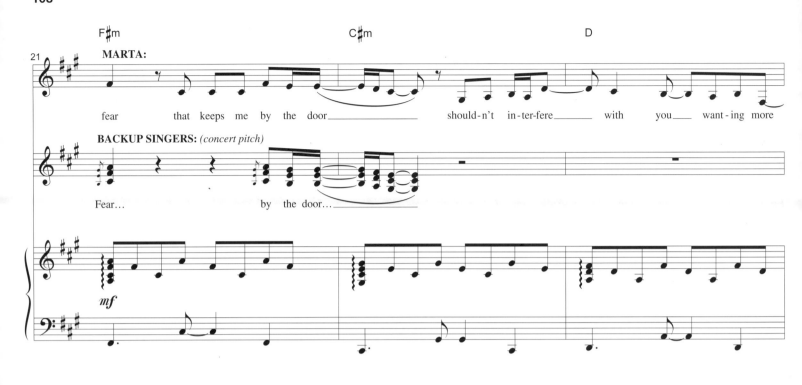

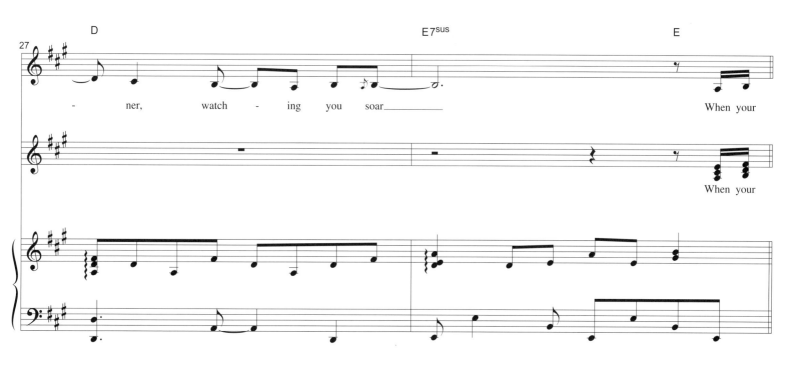

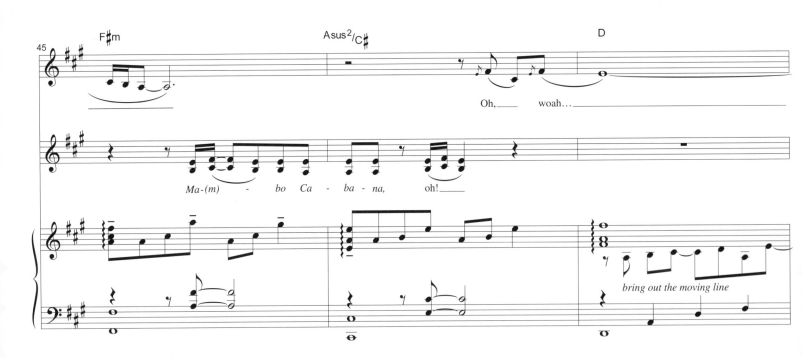

114

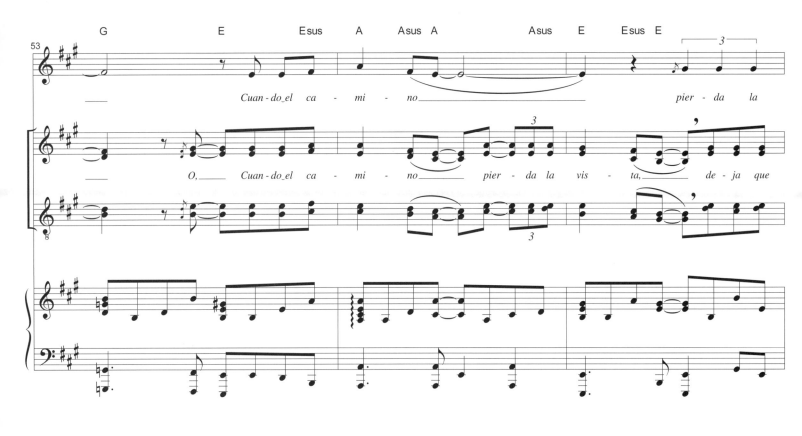

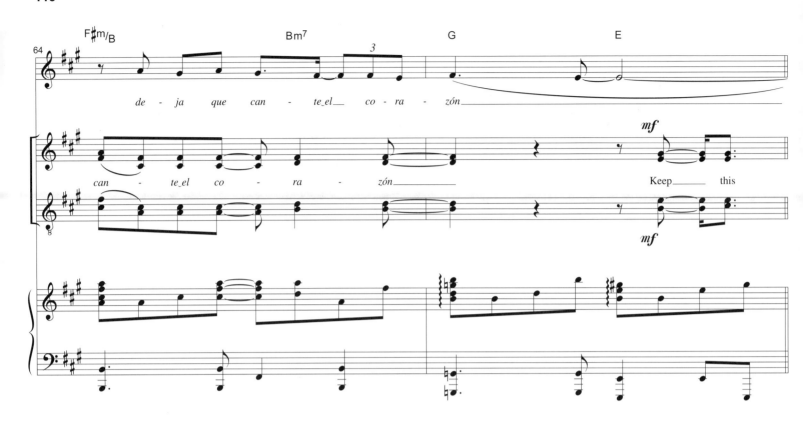

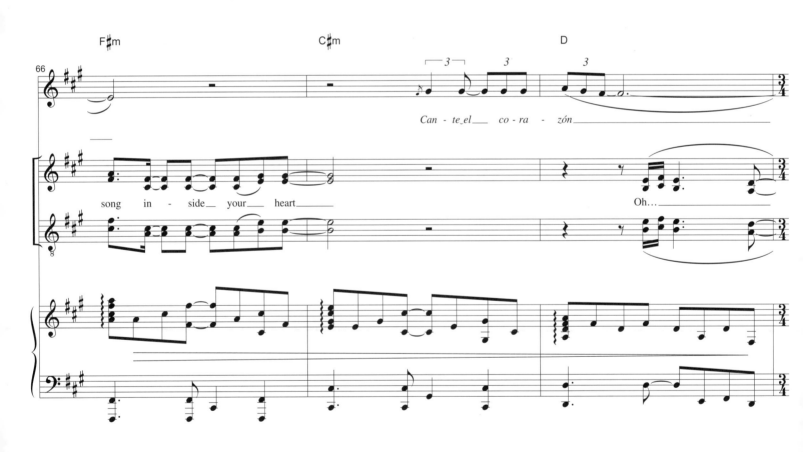

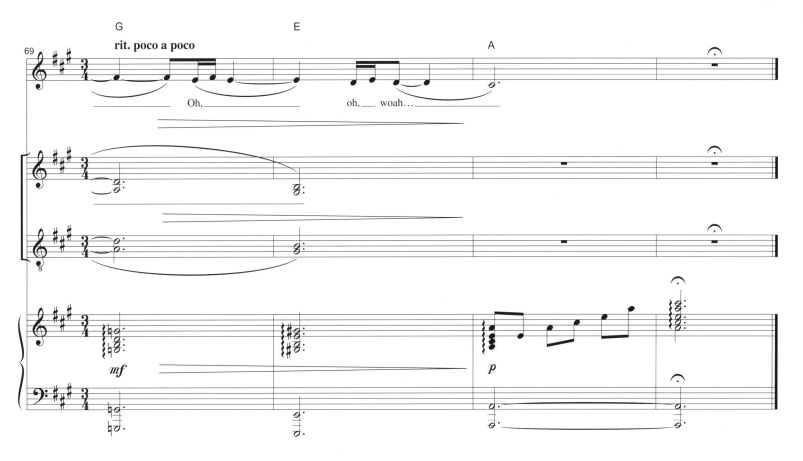

IT WON'T BE LONG NOW

from IN THE HEIGHTS

Music and Lyrics by LIN-MANUEL MIRANDA
Arrangement by ALEX LACAMOIRE
and BILL SHERMAN

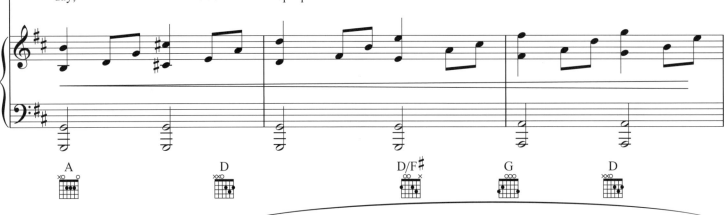

honk - ing at ___ me from ___ his Chev - ro - let! _____ One ___

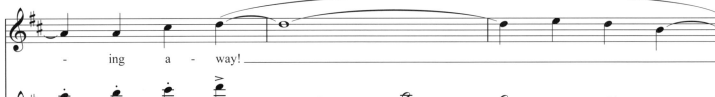

day, I'm hop-pin' in a lim-ou-sine ___ and I'm driv-

- ing a - way! _____

It won't ___

IT'S ALL HAPPENING

from BRING IT ON

Music and Lyrics by
LIN-MANUEL MIRANDA
Arranged by ALEX LACAMOIRE
and TOM KITT

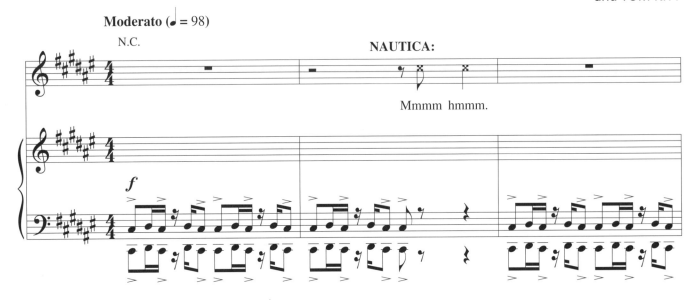

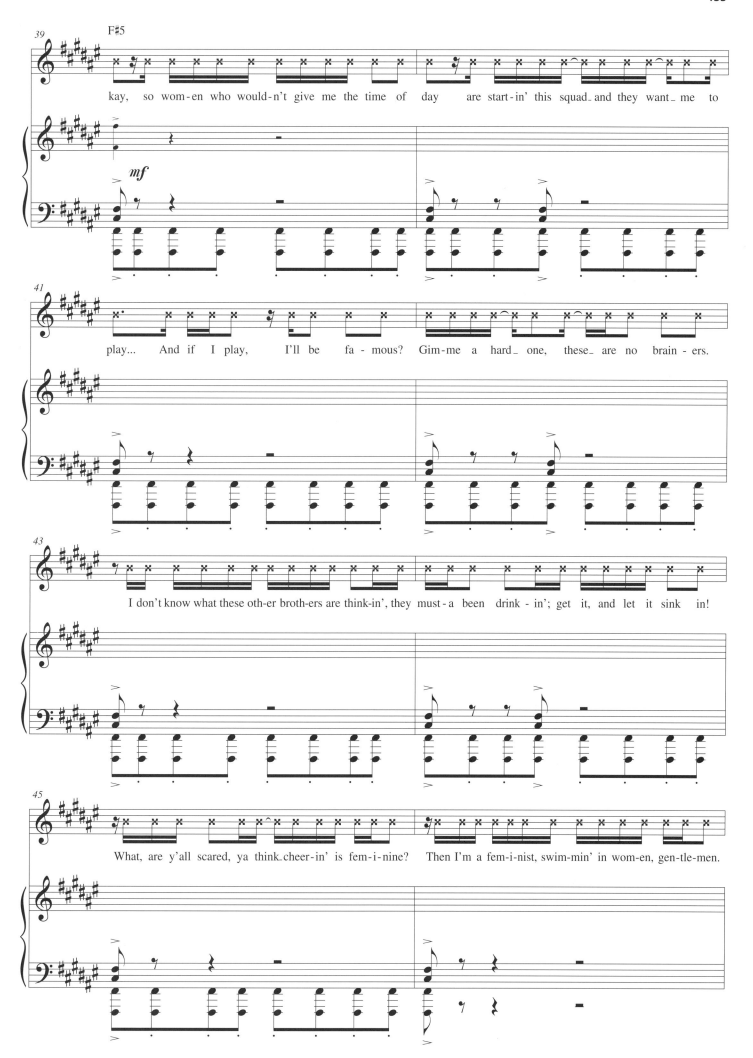

CAMERON: "Stop lying."
CAMPBELL: "'Michael Jordan was a member of the Laney High School cheerleading squad for two years before joining the Junior Varsity Basketball team!'..."

140

KEEP THE BEAT

from the feature film VIVO

Music and Lyrics by
LIN-MANUEL MIRANDA

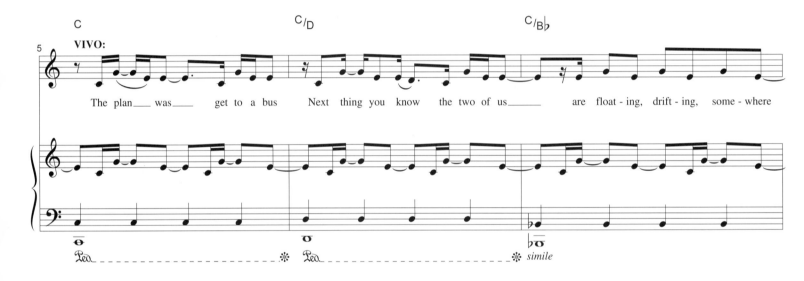

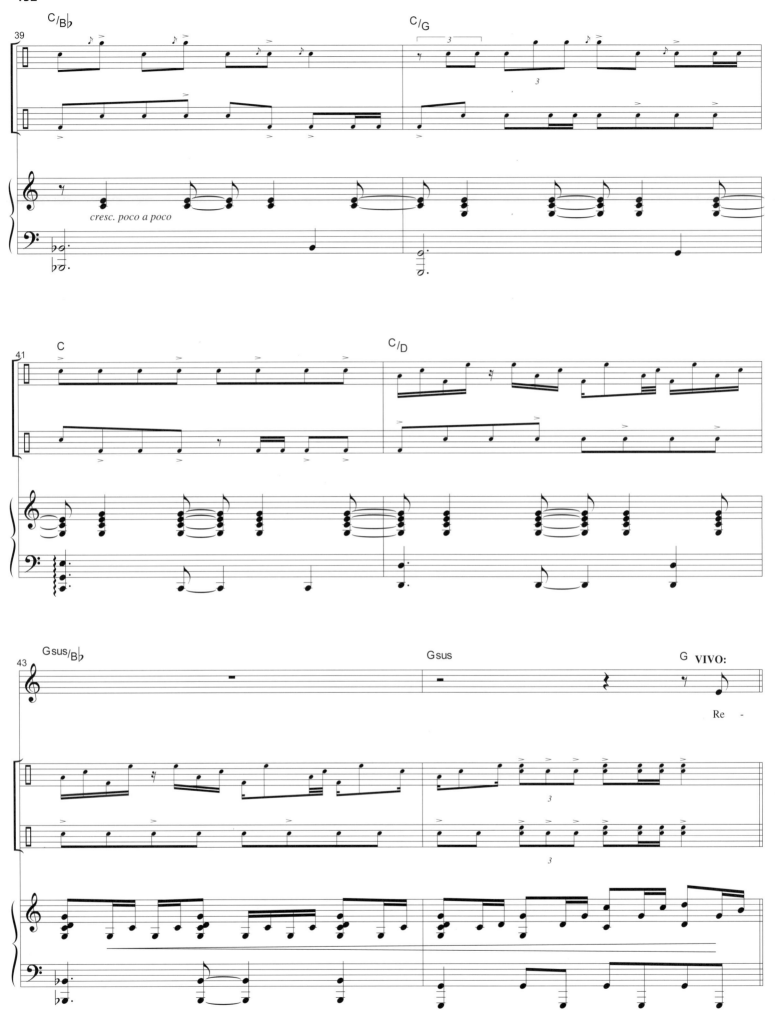

MY OWN DRUM

from the feature film VIVO

Music and Lyrics by
LIN-MANUEL MIRANDA

bounce___ to the beat of my own drum! I'm a wow___ in a world full of ho-hum! I'm a

VOCAL FX: Hey! Hey!

DRUM BEAT

wild___ young la-dy, but you know 'sum? I'd ra-ther be at home with my own___ drum! I

Hey!

Wooh!

MARCHING DRUMS

LOW DRUMS/SNARE

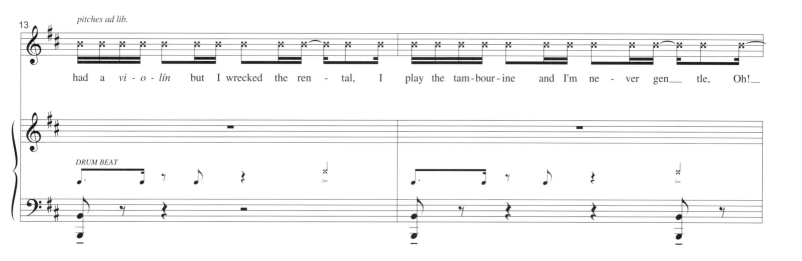

pitches ad lib.

had a vi-o-lín but I wrecked the ren-tal, I play the tam-bour-ine and I'm ne-ver gen___ tle, Oh!___

DRUM BEAT

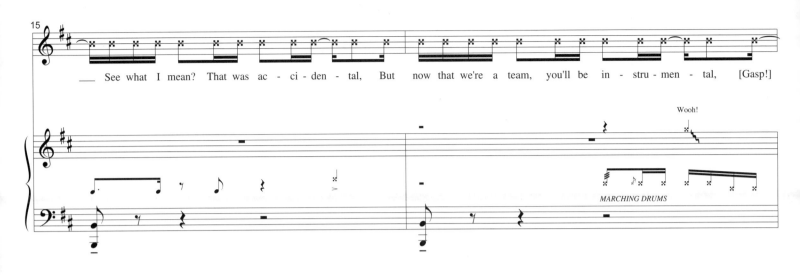

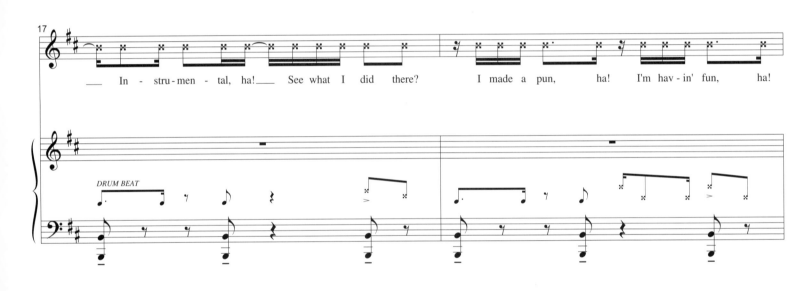

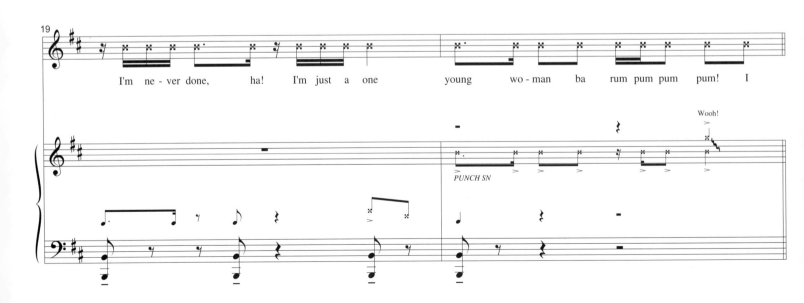

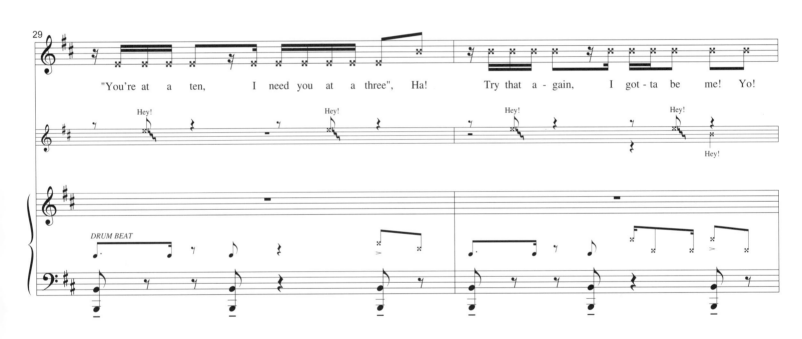

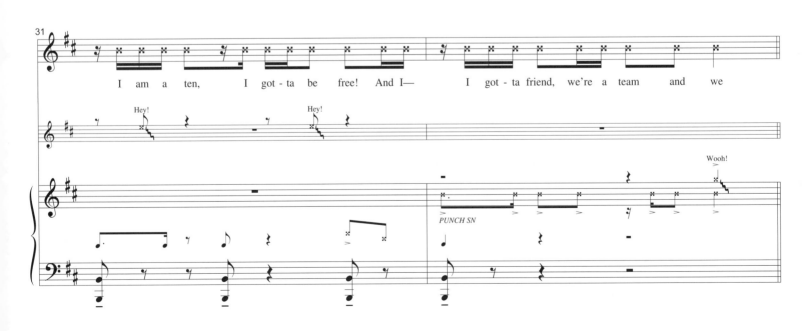

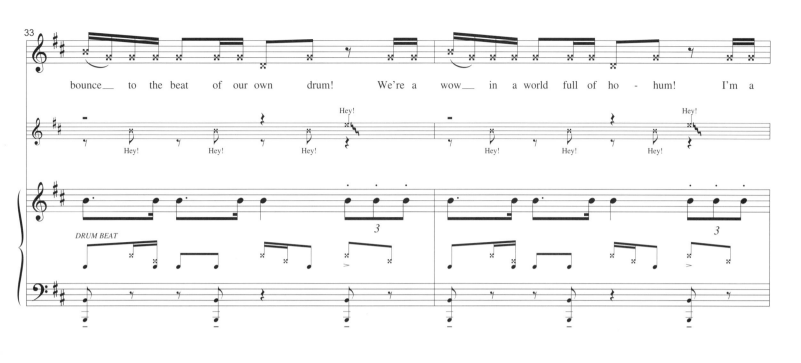

bounce__ to the beat of our own drum! We're a wow__ in a world full of ho - hum! I'm a

wild__ young la - dy, but you know 'sum? I'd ra - ther be at home with my own__ drum! So - lo!

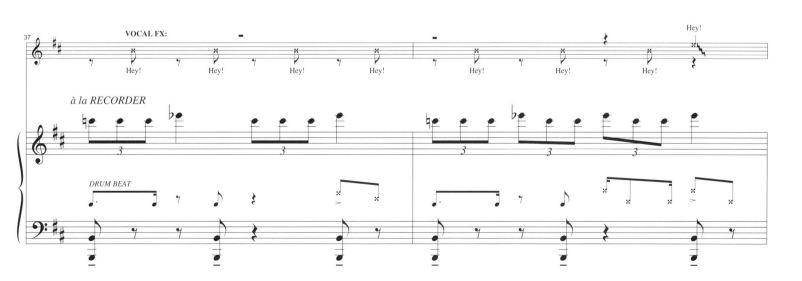

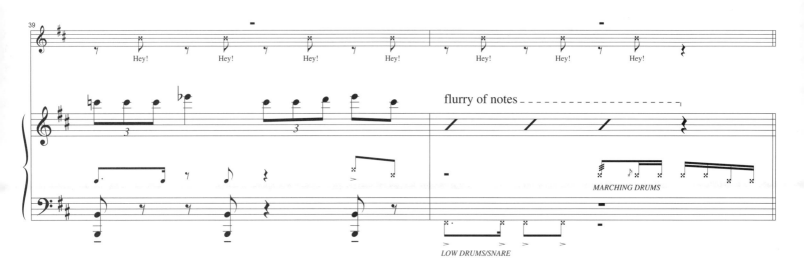

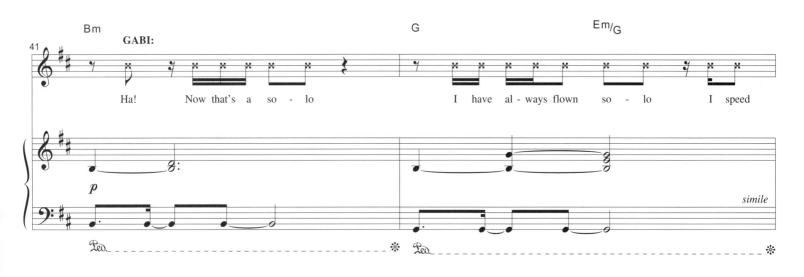

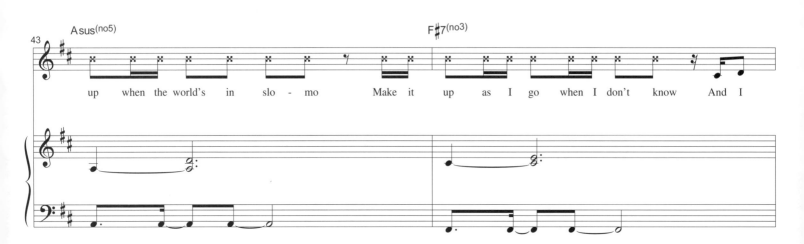

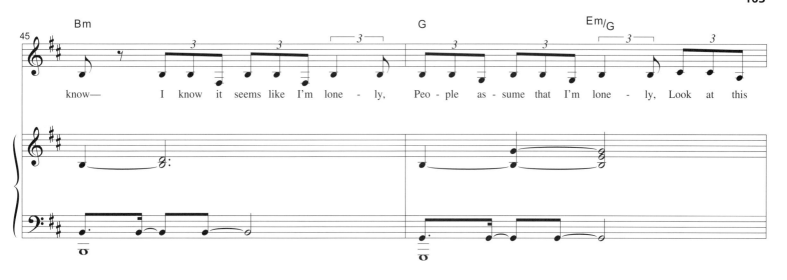

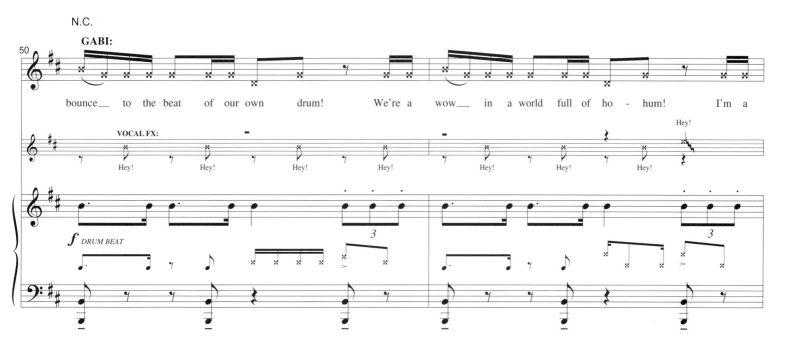

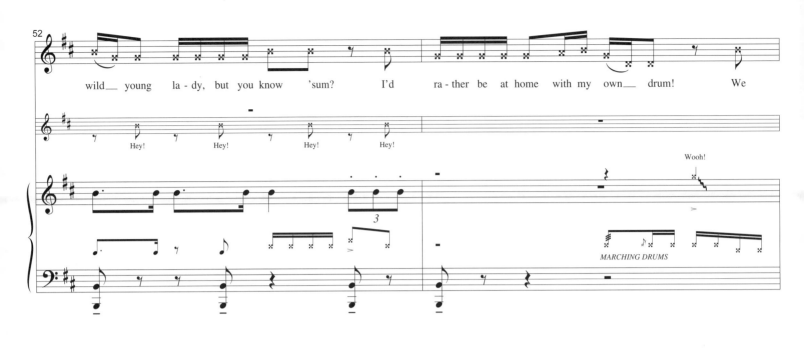

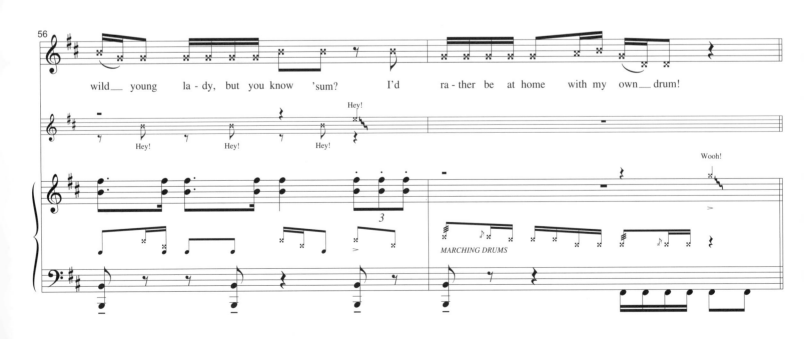

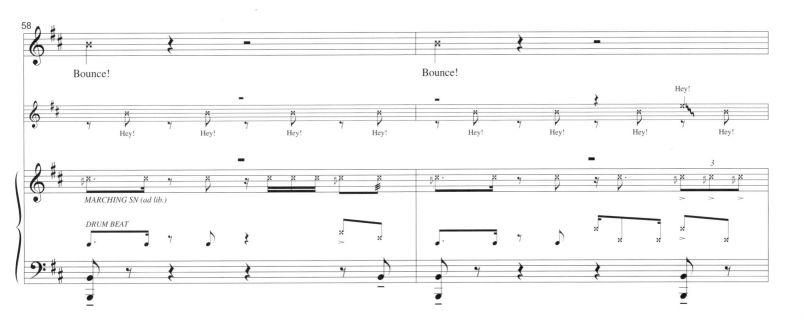

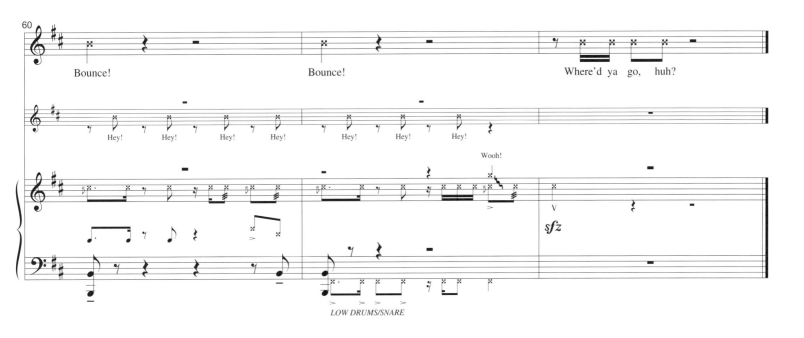

MY SHOT

from HAMILTON

Words and Music by LIN-MANUEL MIRANDA
with Albert Johnson, Kejuan Waliek Muchita,
Osten Harvey, Jr., Roger Troutman
and Christopher Wallace

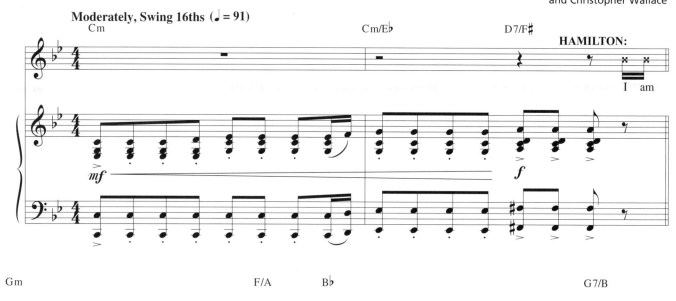

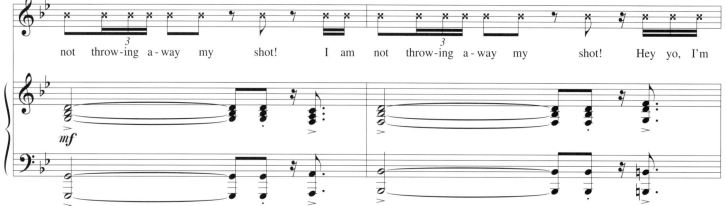

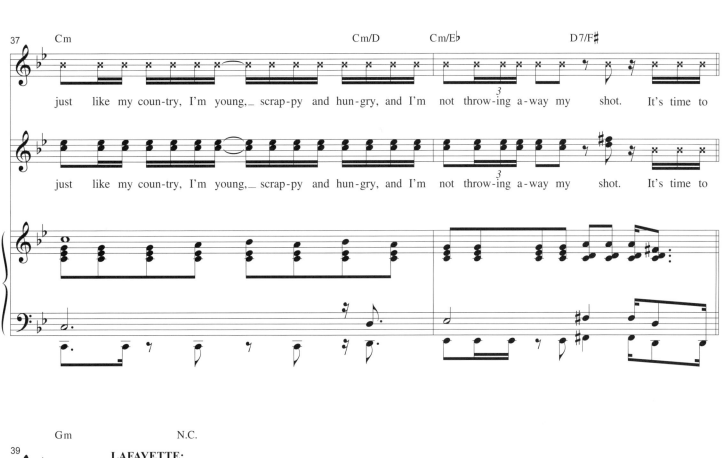

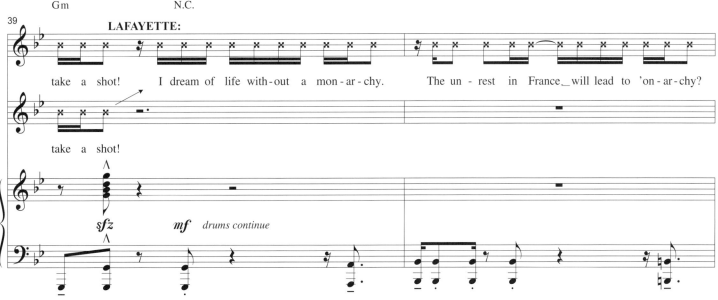

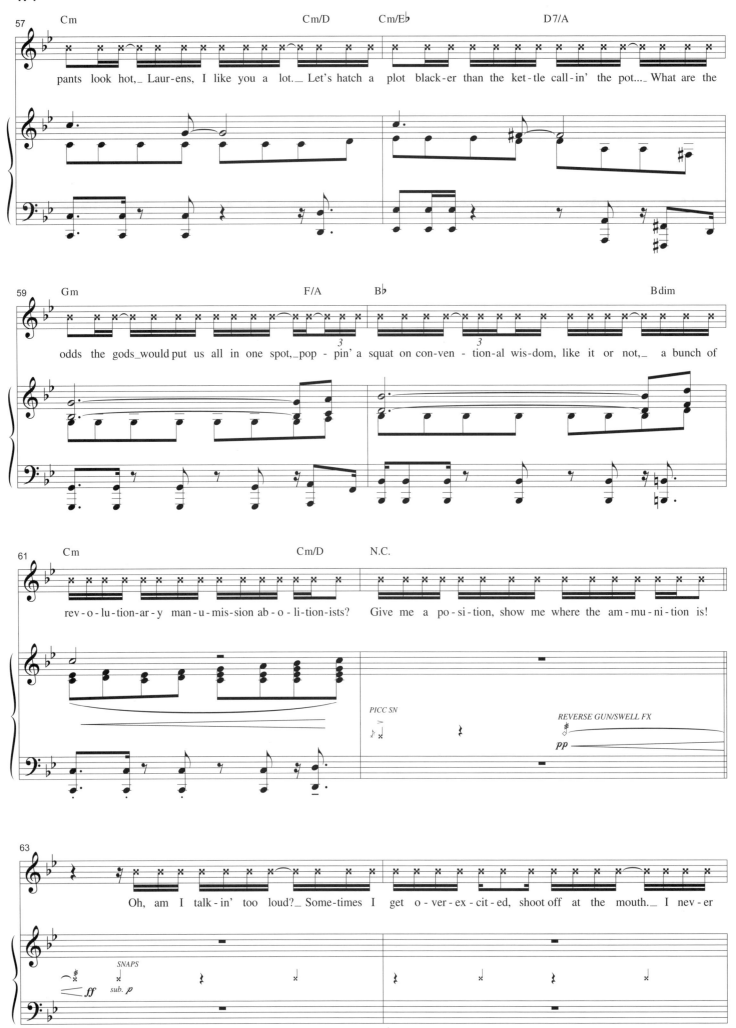

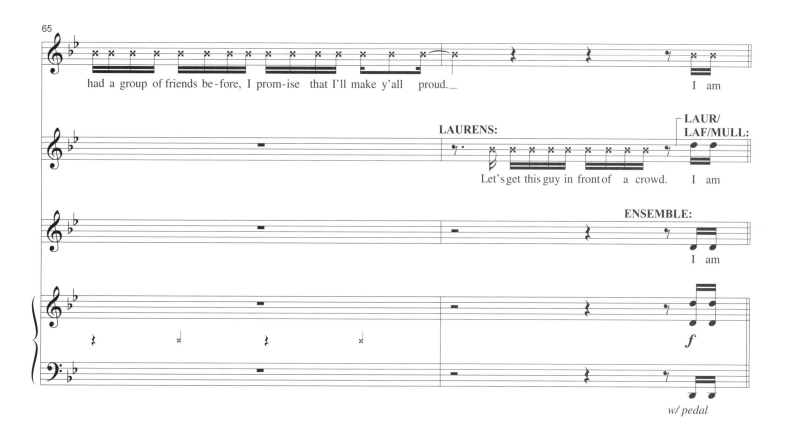

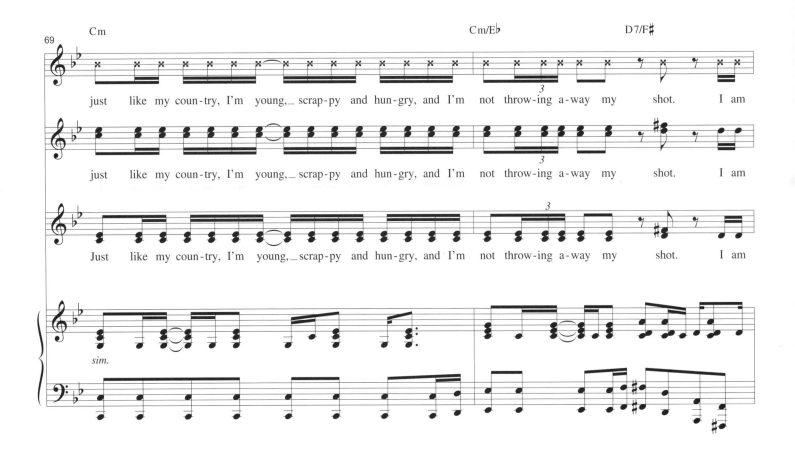

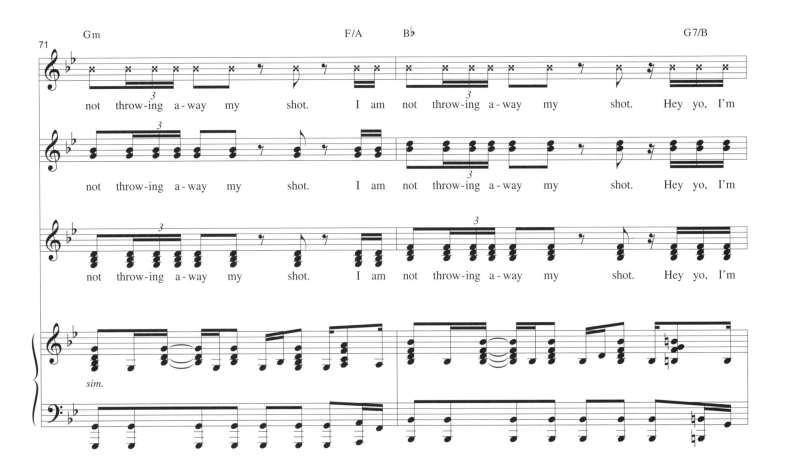

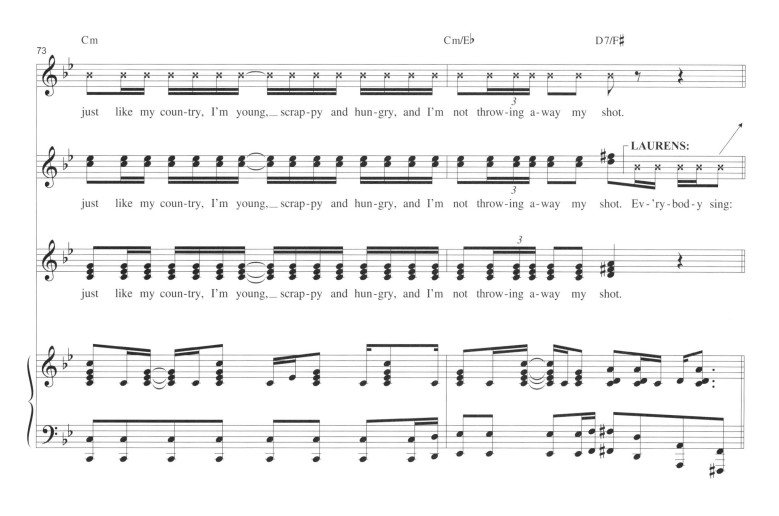

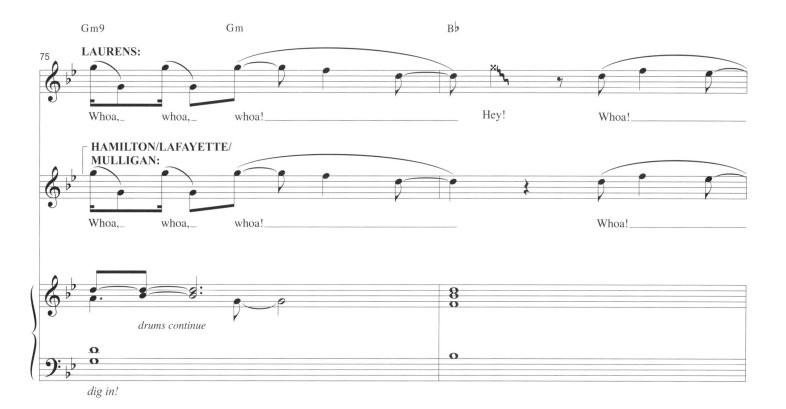

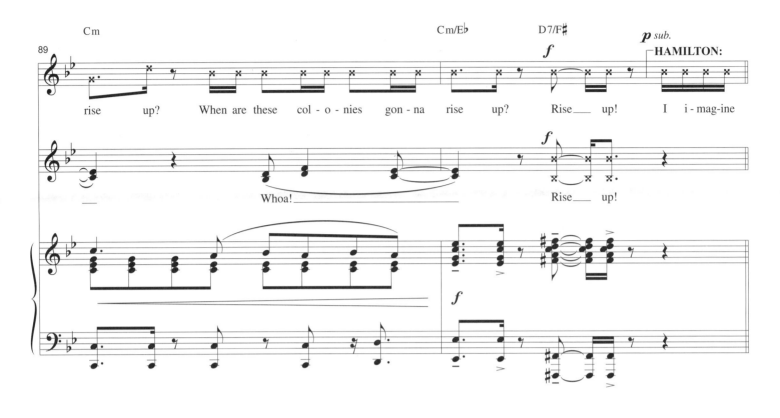

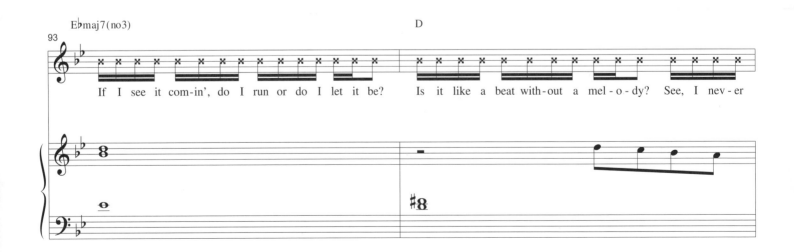

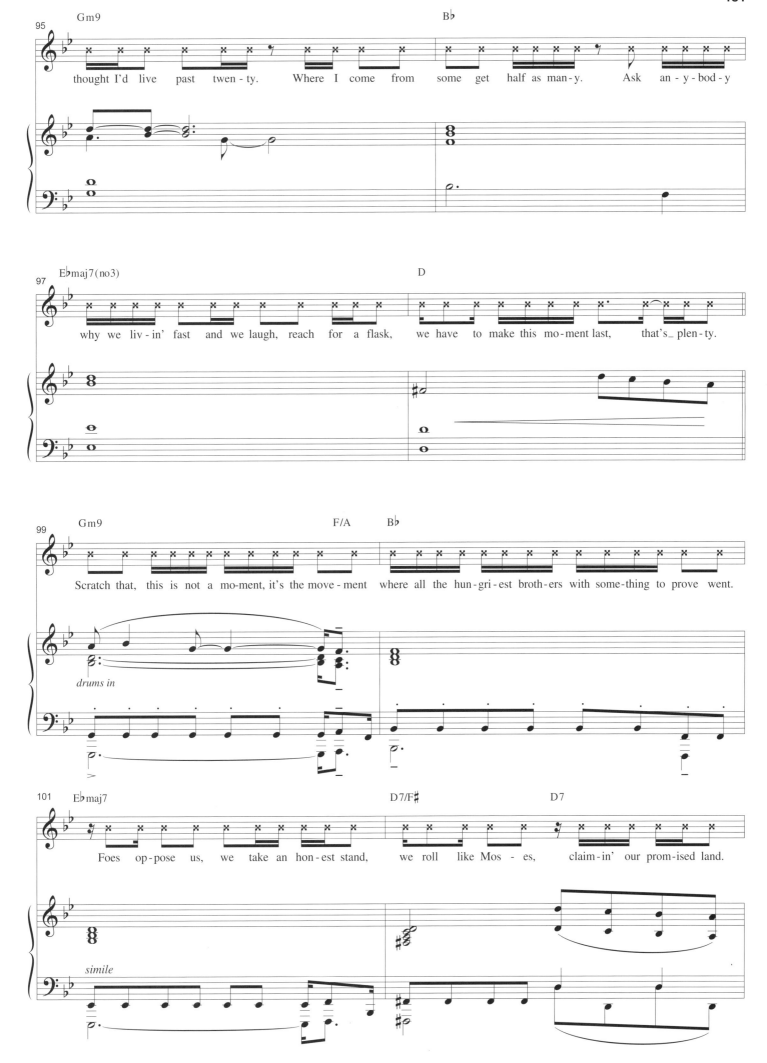

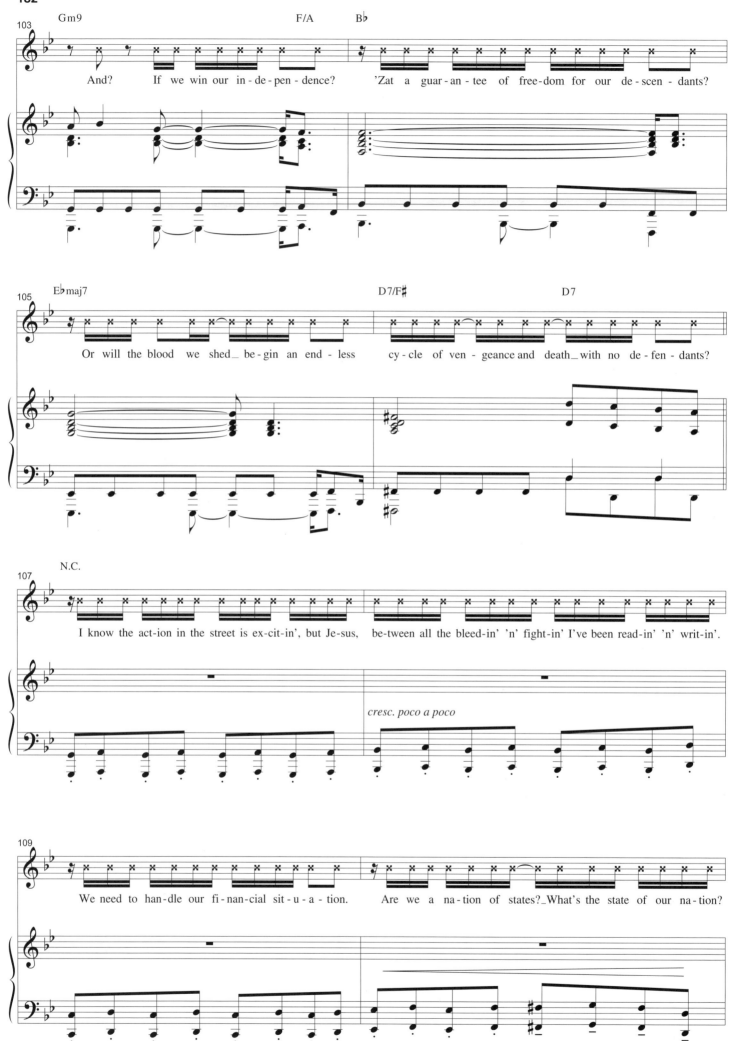

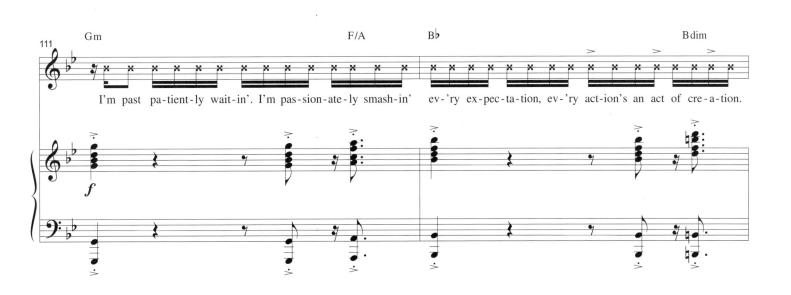

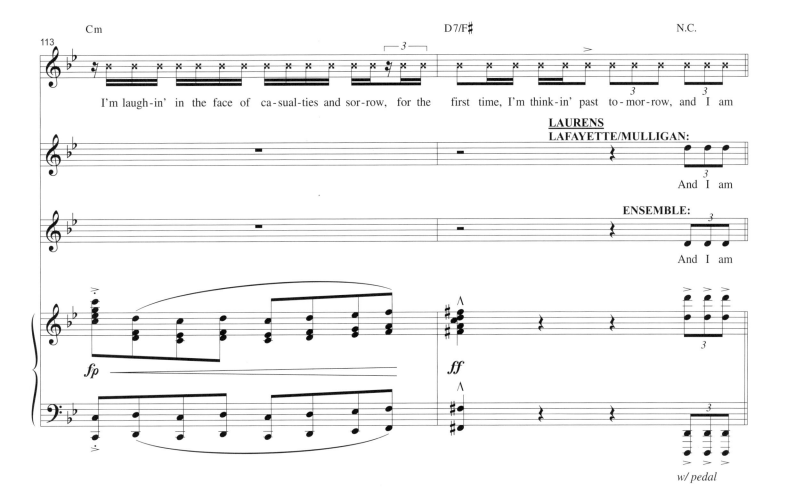

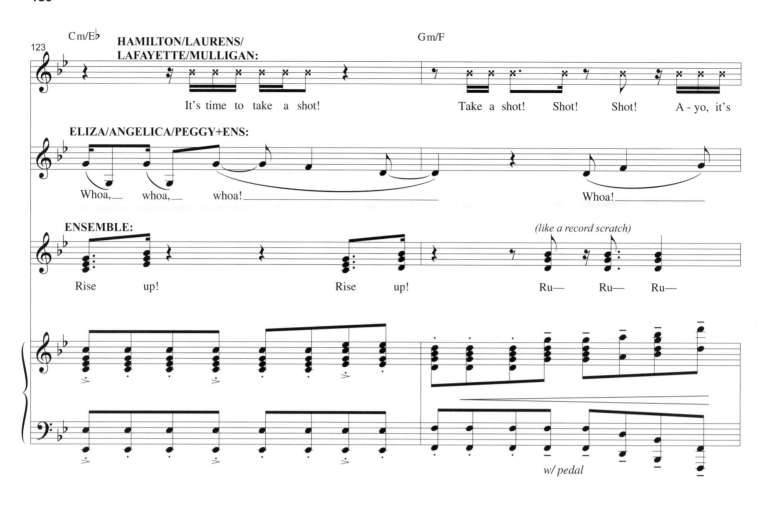

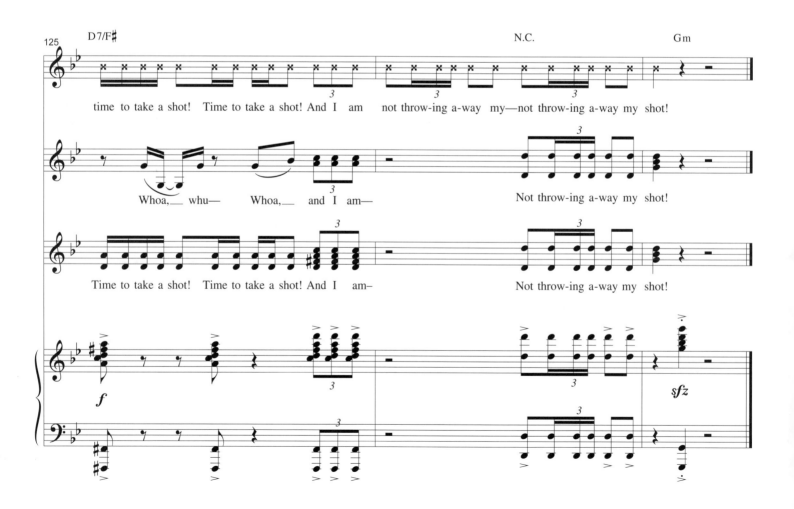

ONE SCHOOL
from 21 CHUMP STREET

Words and Music by
LIN-MANUEL MIRANDA

Moderately

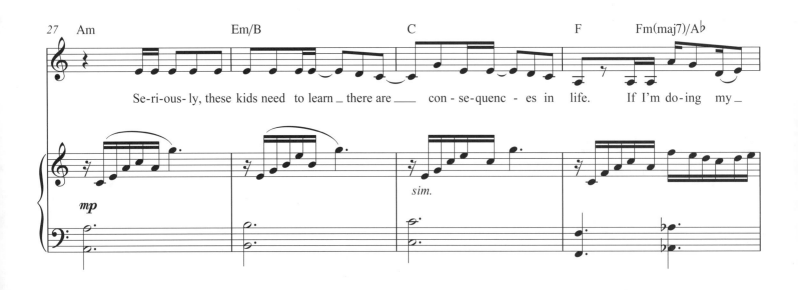

true you make friends on the job, ___ then it ends. You meet kids who are sen-si-tive, smart, and de-fense-less.

Those are the ones you re-mem - ber, ___ the ones that you ___ think a-bout af - ter you're ___ gone.

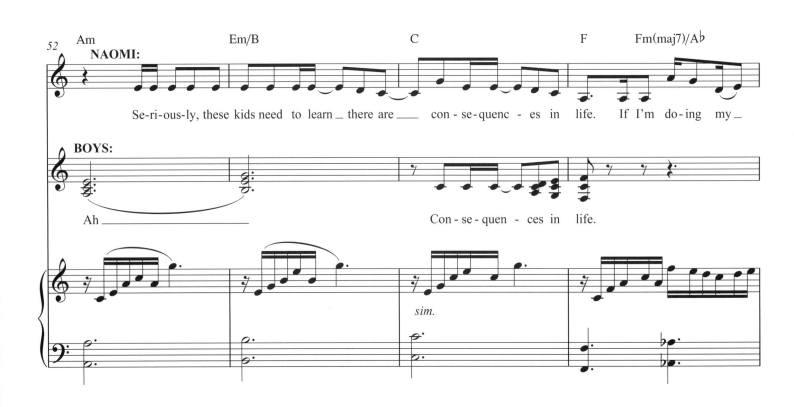

NAOMI:
Se-ri-ous-ly, these kids need to learn ___ there are ___ con-se-quenc - es in life. If I'm do-ing my ___

BOYS:
Ah _____
Con - se - quen - ces in life.

96,000

from IN THE HEIGHTS

Music and Lyrics by LIN-MANUEL MIRANDA
Arrangement by ALEX LACAMOIRE
and BILL SHERMAN

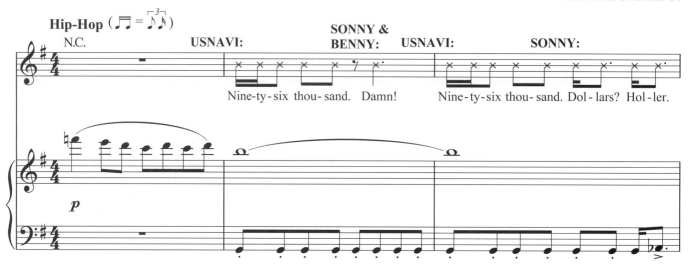

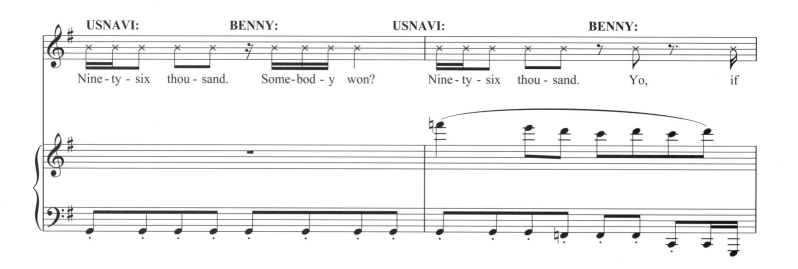

-ter - y, _____ you'll won - der where _ I've been. _____
_____ slow down the high-way of life _ with no _____ re - grets, and no break-in' your neck _

_____ for re-spect or a pay-check. For real _ though, I'll take a break from the wheel and we'll _

USNAVI:
Yo! It's sil - ly when we get in - to these cra-zy hy - po - thet - i - cals, you

_____ I'll be _____ down -

SONNY, DANIELA & ENSEMBLE:
Nine-ty-six thou - sand!

CARLA:
No me di - ga!

mf

202

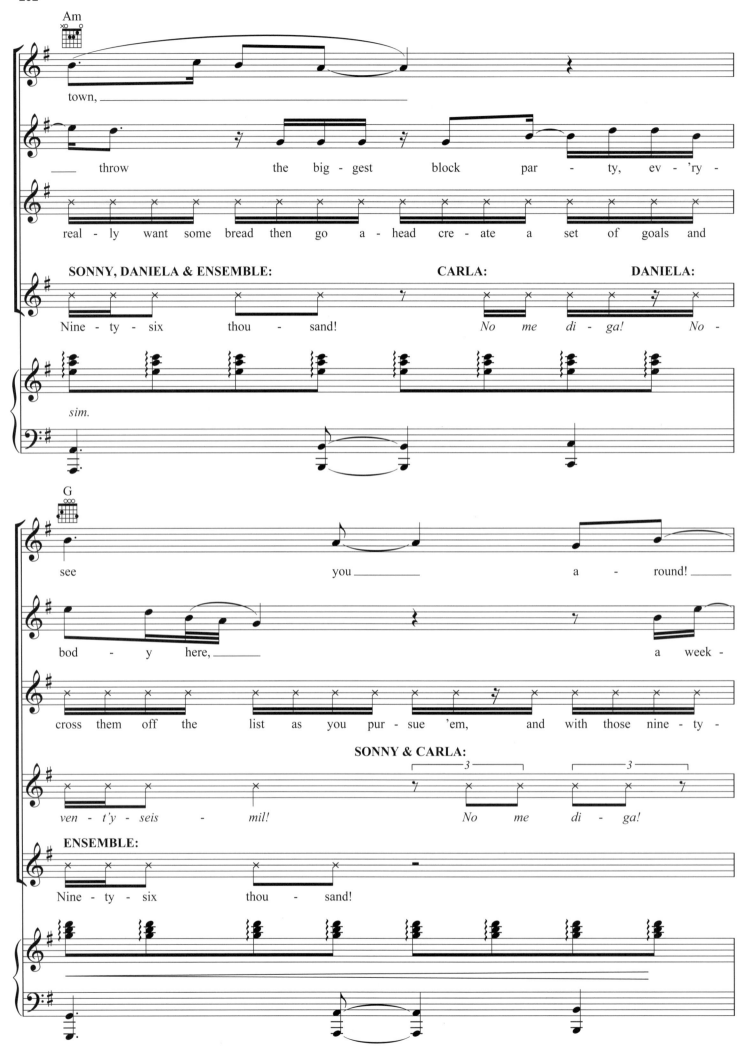

205

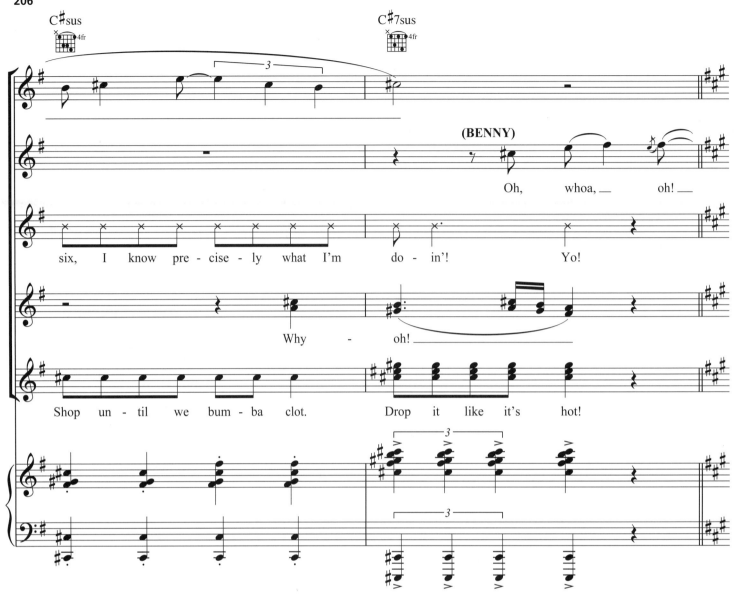

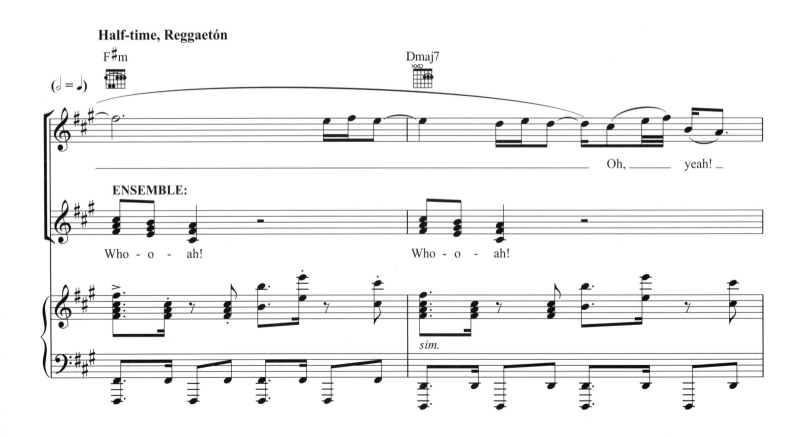

ONE PERFECT MOMENT

from BRING IT ON

Music by TOM KITT
Lyrics by AMANDA GREEN
and LIN-MANUEL MIRANDA

Freely, but with slight urgency

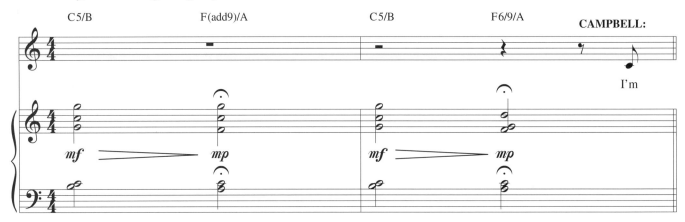

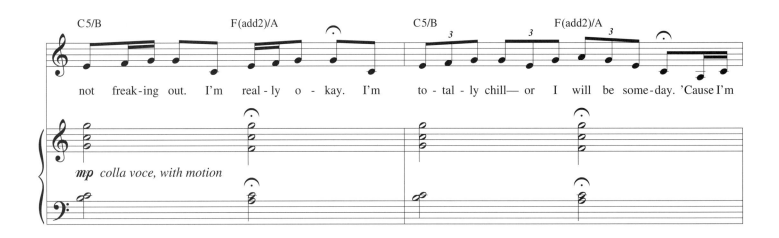

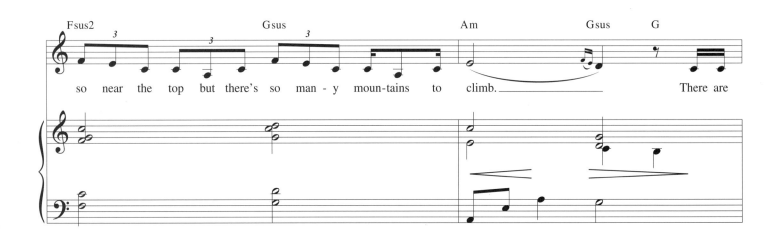

THE SCHUYLER SISTERS
from HAMILTON

Words and Music by
LIN-MANUEL MIRANDA

Funky (♩= 102)

OLD-SCHOOL VINYL HIT

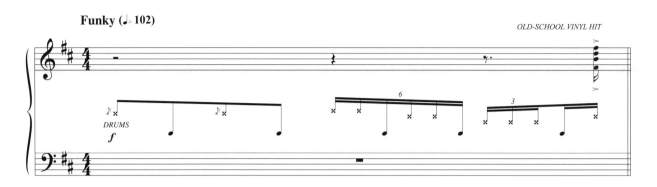

DRUMS

BURR:

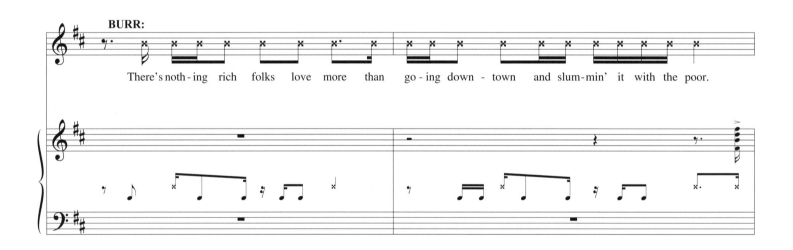

There's noth-ing rich folks love more than go-ing down-town and slum-min' it with the poor.

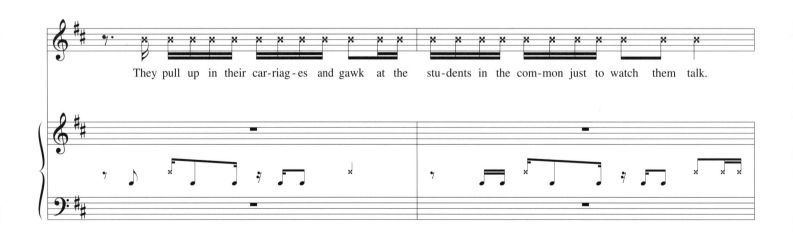

They pull up in their car-riag-es and gawk at the stu-dents in the com-mon just to watch them talk.

Take Phil-ip Schuy-ler: the man is load-ed. Uh-oh, but lit-tle does he know that his

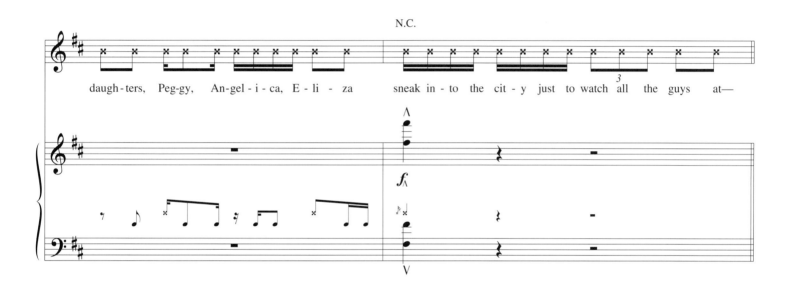

daugh-ters, Peg-gy, An-gel-i-ca, E-li-za sneak in-to the cit-y just to watch all the guys at—

ANGELICA: An-gel-i-ca!
PEGGY: And
ELIZA: E-li-za!
ENSEMBLE: Work, work! Work, work!

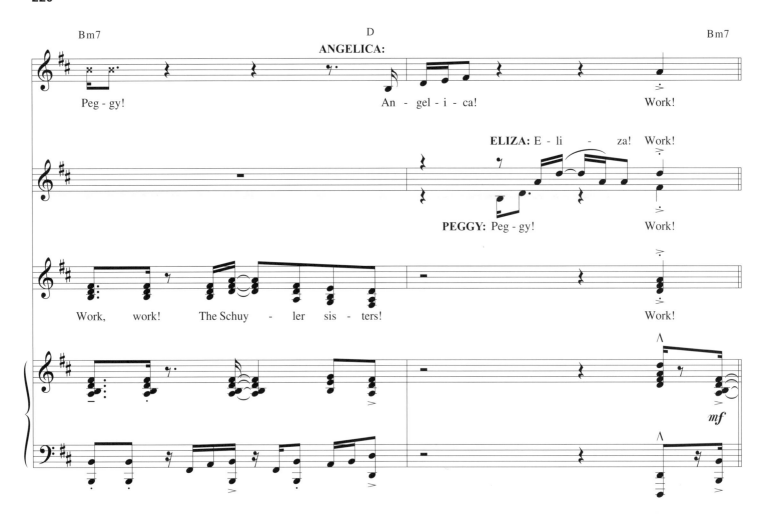

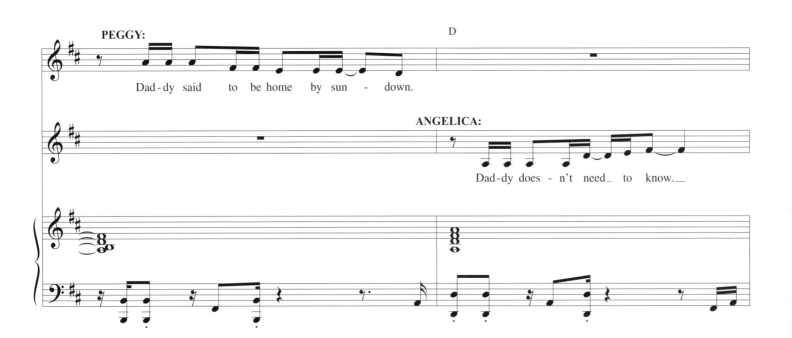

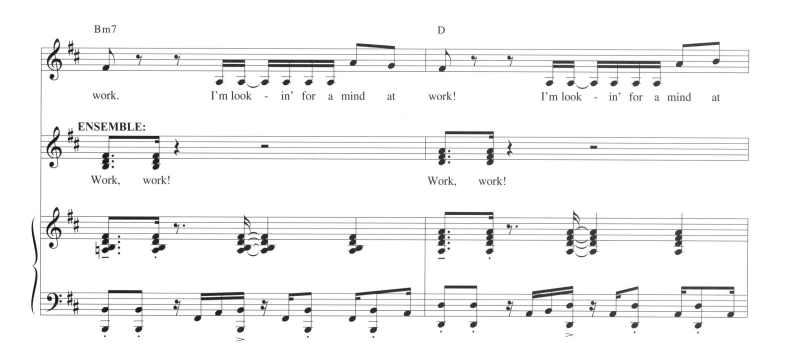

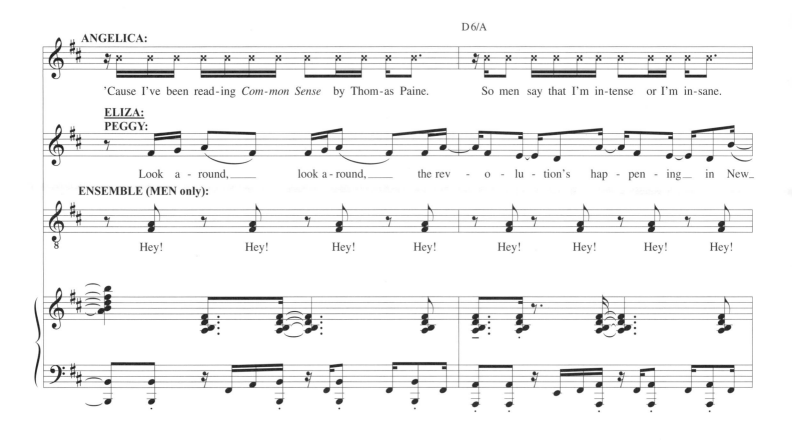

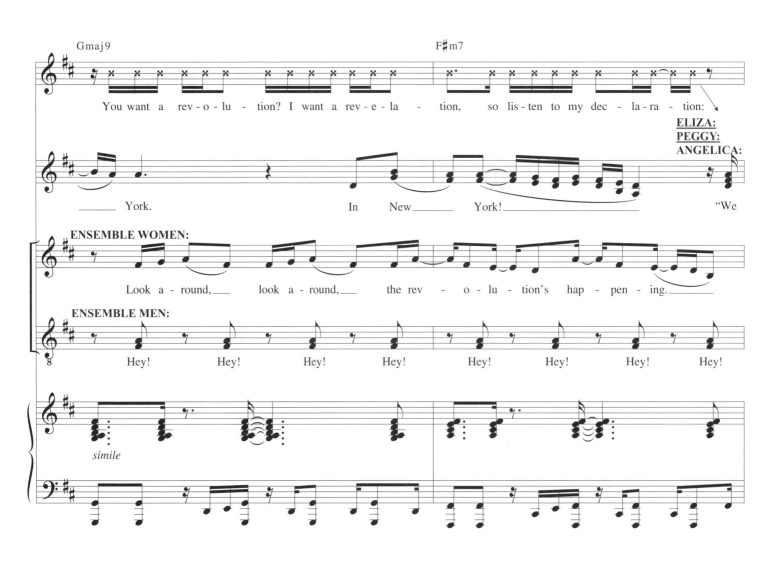

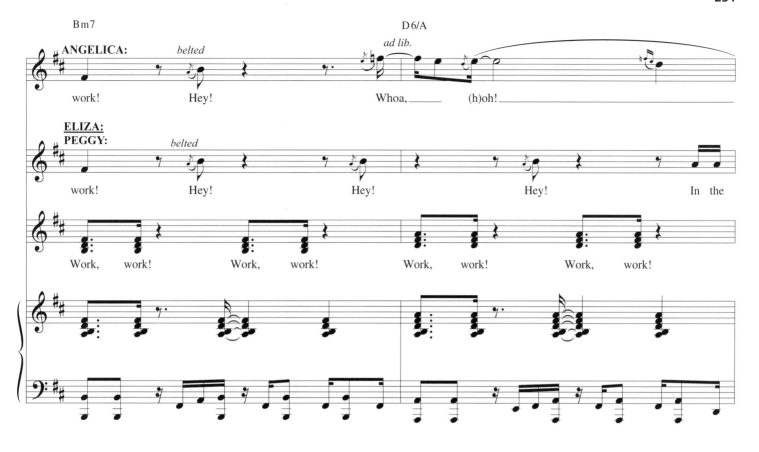

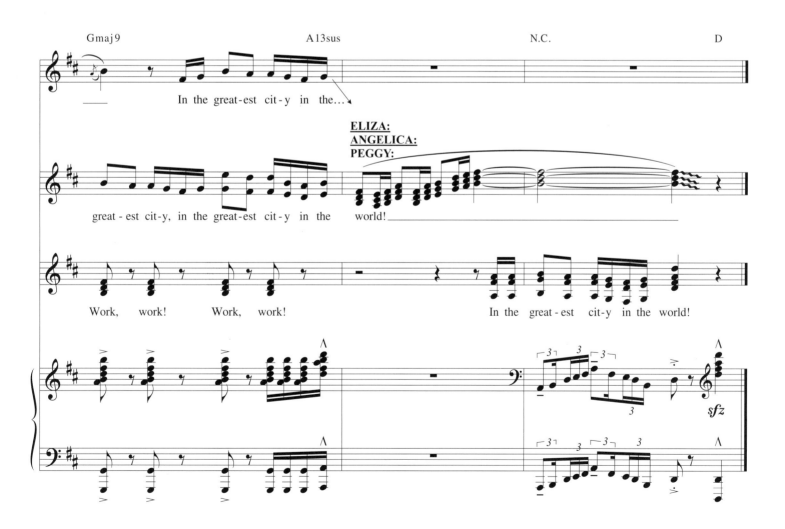

SURFACE PRESSURE

from ENCANTO

Music and Lyrics by
LIN-MANUEL MIRANDA

Moderate Pop

I'm the strong one, I'm not nerv-ous,

I'm as tough as the crust of the earth is.   I move moun-tains, I move church-es,

And I glow, 'cuz I know what my worth is.

* Vocal sung one octave lower than written.

* *Sung at pitch*

WE DON'T TALK ABOUT BRUNO

from ENCANTO

Music and Lyrics by
LIN-MANUEL MIRANDA

Vocal sung an octave lower than written.

Vocal sung an octave lower than written.

250

* *Vocal sung at pitch.*

WHAT ELSE CAN I DO?

from ENCANTO

Music and Lyrics by
LIN-MANUEL MIRANDA

Moderately fast

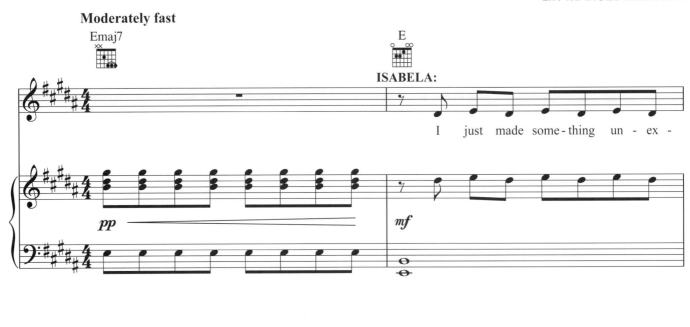

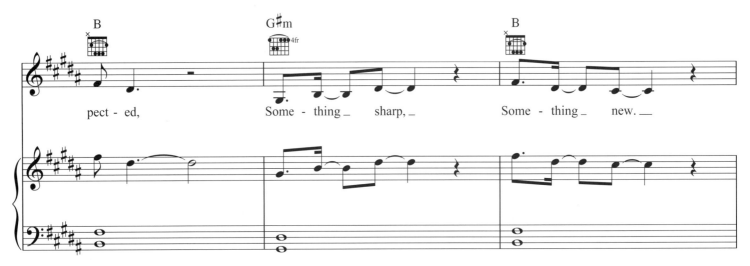

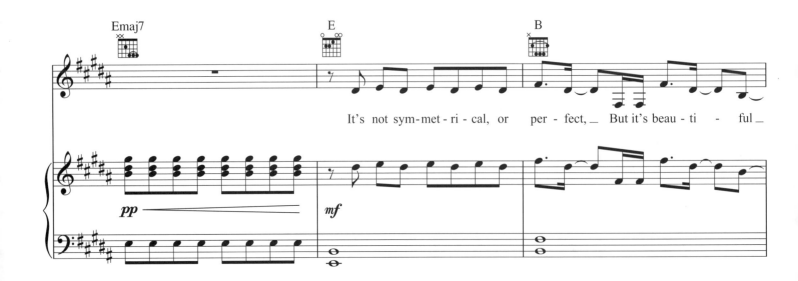

I make per - fect, prac - ticed pos - es. So much hides _ be - hind _

_ my smile. ____ What could I do if I just

grew what I was feel - ing in the mo - ment? _ Do you know _

MIRABEL:

_ where you're go - ing? Whoa... What could I do if I just

ISABELA:

261

WHAT THE HECK I GOTTA DO

from 21 CHUMP STREET

Words and Music by
LIN-MANUEL MIRANDA

Lightly swung 16ths

NARRATOR: *The Plan was called Operation D Minus, and one of the schools included in the plan was Park Vista Community High School, where a kid named Justin Laboi–*

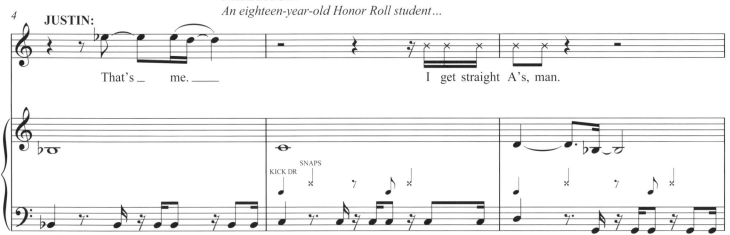

NARRATOR:
An eighteen-year-old Honor Roll student...

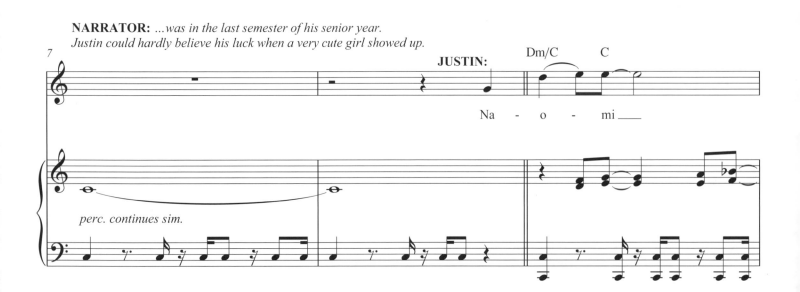

NARRATOR: *...was in the last semester of his senior year.*
Justin could hardly believe his luck when a very cute girl showed up.

NARRATOR: *You told her all this in class?*
JUSTIN: *Well, I texted her, yeah.*

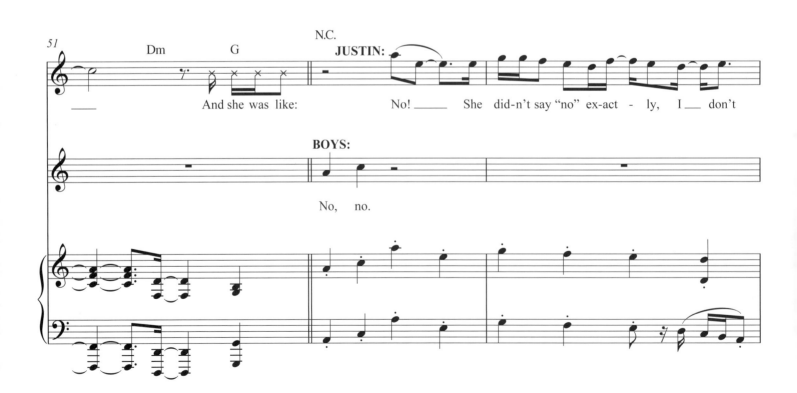

NARRATOR: *You asked her to the prom?*
JUSTIN: *Yeah, I danced and everything!*

WHERE YOU ARE

from MOANA

Music by LIN-MANUEL MIRANDA,
OPETAIA FOA'I and MARK MANCINA
Lyrics by LIN-MANUEL MIRANDA

YOU'LL BE BACK

from HAMILTON

Words and Music by
LIN-MANUEL MIRANDA

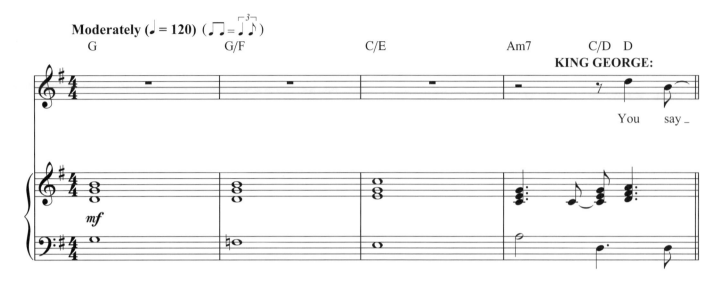

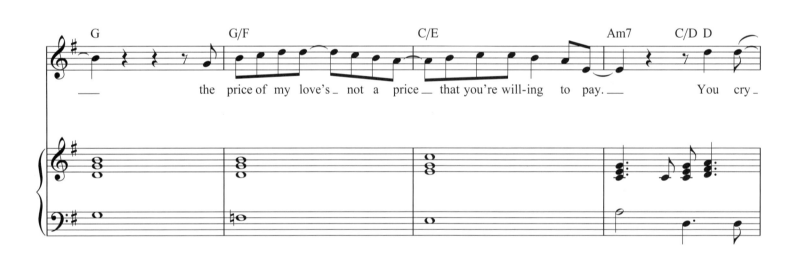

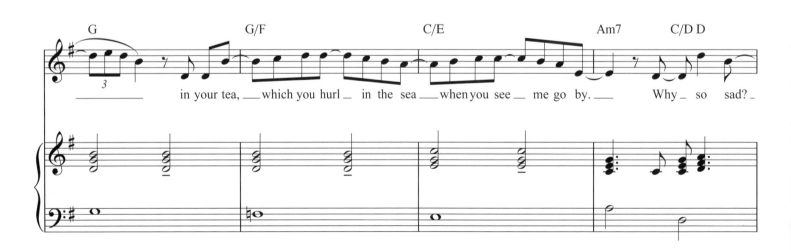

YOU'RE WELCOME

from MOANA

Music and Lyrics by
LIN-MANUEL MIRANDA

Additional Lyrics

Rap: Kid, honestly, I could go on and on.
I could explain ev'ry nat'ral phenomenon.
The tide? The grass? The ground?
Oh, that was Maui, just messing around.

I killed an eel, I buried its guts,
Sprouted a tree: now you got coconuts!
What's the lesson? What is the takeaway?
Don't mess with Maui when he's on a breakaway.

And the tapestry here in my skin
Is a map of the vict'ries I win!
Look where I've been! I make ev'rything happen!
Look at that mean mini Maui, just tickety
Tappin'! Heh, heh, heh,
Heh, heh, heh, hey!